Secrets
BEYOND THE GRAVE

Dwight Hall

Remnant Publications, Inc.
Coldwater, MI

Cover photos by
Brandx Pictures and Stockbyte

Cover Design by
David Berthiaume

Secrets Beyond the Grave
This edition published 2005

Printed in the United States of America

ISBN 1-883012-36-8

ARE YOU SEARCHING?

Reliable, Commonsense Answers for Your Urgent Questions

- ☑ *Can you have real peace in a world of chaos and violence?*
- ☑ *How can you have lifelong good health?*
- ☑ *What really happens to you after death?*
- ☑ *How can you have better relationships with family and friends?*
- ☑ *Can you know and understand the future?*

*W*ith all the crime, violence, and economic insecurity, are you searching for truth that will give you lasting peace? You can find the answers you need to these and other vital questions by enrolling in our FREE Bible study course. These eye-opening, thought-provoking lessons will give the straightforward answers that millions have used to improve their lives—without being "preachy."

Better yet, you won't be told what the Bible says about life after death, hell and prophecy, you'll be *shown* with hundreds of verses that will help you understand the Bible for yourself. You'll discover the tried and true tools to make the best decisions today, and make a better future for you and your family tomorrow!

Do You Want Answers?

Yes! Please send me, at no charge, the first two lessons.

Name _____

Address _____

City _____ State _____ Zip _____

Send to:

**Bible Correspondence Course
P.O. Box 426
Coldwater, MI 49036**   SBG

Preface

Sharing truth isn't, or at least shouldn't be, about making money, but helping people recognize those things that are most important in this life. Quite simply, that means forsaking a lifestyle based on turning a profit and accepting one based on turning heads and changing lives, *whatever the final cost.*

We're living in a time when this kind of philosophy is difficult to practice. Not only is truth forsaken for fantasy, but often if something doesn't meet the bottom line, it's tossed aside as invaluable. Moreover, innovation costs money and time that people concerned with sharing Bible truth don't often have; yet if you're not innovating, you're not reaching enough people.

Quite frankly, I want to be innovative about sharing truth, which is the purpose of this book. Interest in the supernatural and paranormal is exploding in every possible way—from television, to books, to Hollywood films, to psychic networks, and more. With pop culture and so many outspoken religions focusing in on the afterlife, I can't fathom how the busy dad, mom, or child has the time to stop and get the plain truth.

When my niece Katie died, I needed this truth. I was confused, and I saw how this same confusion hurt others. But most people see the ultimate truth about the afterlife as something that can wait—until they're dead. But this isn't the case at all; according to the Bible, knowing about what happens when you die is nearly as important as knowing how you should live.

So I was convicted to find a way to teach confused people and curious souls what God really has to say about the spirit world, things I learned from years of study, using innovative ideas that speak to today's busy reader. I consulted good writers and lobbied the ideas of experts to facilitate innovation . . . and it worked.

Ultimately, I realized the detailed truth has already been said the best way possible by someone else. So instead of reinventing the wheel, I decided the best approach was to give you the same exact looking glass the Christian church had just a few hundred years ago. Thus this book presents the commentary of one of Christianity's most prolific and respected writers the world has ever known—Ellen White, whose classic *The Great Controversy* is the framework of this effort. So much for innovation!

Still, the real challenge was not presenting new information and backing it up with new evidence or new interpretations of Scripture, but rather being able to say something quite old and fundamental in a unique fashion . . . in a way that people today can grasp quickly in their busy lives. So my part in this book is simply to lead you through valuable, biblically sound information as old as history.

I've basically teamed up with my favorite author to share with you the plain Bible truth about what happens when we die—in a way you can digest without spending hours of time you just don't have. But whatever time you give to this journey will be worth it. It is a journey that will blow you away . . . not just because you will probably learn something new, but even better, because you will learn something that changes your life, gives you amazing joy, and prepares you for the future.

The cost of sharing truth can be brutal—but I'm willing to sacrifice to achieve that end. But the cost I can't accept is failure. I'm willing to lose money and my friends' respect in getting Bible facts into the hands of the common person. If this book makes a million dollars but doesn't change one life, then I've wasted my time. If it changes the lives of countless people with truth, but loses money, you'll see a smile on my face until I die.

How to Read This Book

Since the bulk of this book is material adapted from *The Great Controversy*, but is supplemented with my own material, I've formatted her words differently than mine. For instance, my words will appear like the words on this page, while her adapted commentary will appear in this font:

In the words of the prophet Isaiah, "To the law and to the testimony: if they speak not according to this word, it is because there is no light in them" (Isaiah 8:20).

Finally, after you finish this book, I highly recommend you discover its source material, *The Great Controversy.* I know it will bless you tremendously. Call 800-423-1319 to get your copy.

With that, you're ready to learn the incredible secrets behind what happens when we die. It's an amazing adventure, and God will bless you in your journey for truth.

Dwight Hall
President, Remnant Publications

Acknowledgements

As with most books, it took an entire team of dedicated, hard-working professionals—and not just one writer—to make what's in your hands possible in such a short time. Although my name goes on the cover as the author, I would be terribly remiss if I didn't acknowledge those who worked with my same passion to see this effort through to the end.

Therefore, special thanks goes to:

My niece, Katie, for the inspiration to write this book, and her parents Gary and Heidi and sister Kelsie, for their courage.

My entire hardworking, tireless staff at Remnant Publications, who worked long hours with amazing energy to accomplish a modern-day miracle.

My good friend Jonathan Gibbs, for helping to prepare the project from the start and, most important, his shared conviction about the power of the printed page and getting plain truth into wide circulation.

Cari Haus and Anthony Lester, for their combined writing and editing expertise and their ideas, fine tuning my often rough sketches and turning them into clear, concise copy that has the power to transform lives.

David Berthiaume and Penny Hall, for their creative input, design and work on the cover.

My brother Dan Hall, for formatting the copy up until the moment of press, keeping a sharp eye even into the late evenings.

And my wife, kids, and grandchild, for the inspiration to do what's right and important in this life.

Finally, I must offer my deepest gratitude for the basis of this book, the scriptural writings of E.G. White, especially her classic, *The Great Controversy*. Her works changed my life and continue to fuel my passion to share Bible truth with as many people as possible.

And most important, I gratefully acknowledge God and His Word, the source of all truth and hope in this world.

Contents

1

The Crisis

D wight, are you there?" Linda's quivering voice pleaded over the answering machine. "Oh, God, please let him be there!"

I was dozing off into an afternoon nap when the phone began to ring. Still in that no man's land between sleep and awareness, it took a few moments for the desperation in Linda's voice to jar me out of my lethargy.

"Linda, this is Dwight. What's wrong?"

"Katie was hit by a car!" My wife's mother spoke breathlessly. "It doesn't look very good. Can you meet us at the emergency room?"

"We'll be right there," I hurriedly assured her. Now fully awake, I raced through the house to tell Deb what had happened to our niece. Both horrified, we quickly changed into suitable clothes, bounded downstairs, and nearly fell over ourselves climbing into the car.

On the half mile journey down our driveway, we prayed earnestly that Katie would be okay. Visions of that sweet little bundle of energy, with her shoulder length blonde hair and mischievous blue eyes, flashed into my mind. How could we ever do without her talkative, quick-witted ways? I quickly tried to shut the thought out of my mind. I knew that Katie was accident-prone, having broken a few bones before. But I was sure she would be fine. She had to be.

Katie loved riding her little motorcycle. And as she so often did on a Saturday afternoon, she lugged the bulky dirt bike out of the garage and had her daddy help her start it. Katie then put on her helmet, strapped it tight, and climbed aboard—excited about the ride to come on that clear and beautiful summer day.

Just like she'd done dozens if not hundreds of times before, Katie engaged the throttle and soon felt the warmth of the breeze against her face as the bike surged into motion. As she rode that day, her parents worked in the yard, trusting their little girl to obey their rules of safety.

But then in what seemed like only moments, a van struck her broadside, flinging her body and bike into the air and across the scorching pavement.

Hearing the crash, Katie's parents knew immediately that something was dreadfully wrong. With sounds of the accident still echoing in their ears, they rushed across the yard to check on their little girl.

To their great horror, they found Katie's broken body alone on the road, barely clinging to life.

The tires of our car had barely screeched to a stop in front of the hospital when Deb jumped out and rushed inside. I drove on quickly, looking for a place to park, but I soon noticed Deb running toward me across the parking lot, frantically waving her arms.

"They aren't here," she explained as she jumped back into the car. "A helicopter is flying Katie to the trauma unit in Kalamazoo." As we raced off to her sister's home, I kept thinking about how bad things seemed. If they had to send Katie to a bigger, better equipped hospital, she couldn't be doing too well.

I'll never forget the scene at Gary and Heidi's house. The images still rush through my mind with frightful clarity. The entire area surrounding my sister-in-law's home was in complete commotion, with ambulance lights flashing and police directing traffic. Off in a clearing, a helicopter had already landed. It was as surreal an experience as you can imagine.

When we explained who we were, the police quickly let us through the roadblock. Parking the car, we rushed over to Wendell, Deb's father. His face was covered with shock, grief, and stress.

"Wendell, what happened?"

As Wendell slowly retold details of the tragic accident, I groaned. One of Katie's legs had been crushed. When her father found her, she wasn't even breathing. For uncountable minutes until help arrived,

Gary had to give his little daughter mouth-to-mouth resuscitation. During those moments, Katie hung on the precipice between life and death.

The next thing I knew, the helicopter carrying my niece lifted off the ground and banked toward Kalamazoo. Still in a state of shock, Gary and Heidi climbed into our Ford for the agonizing hour-long drive to the hospital. Even as Deb and I tried to reassure them, concerns for my own children and their safety haunted my thoughts.

By the time we arrived, a chaplain was waiting for us. Shortly after he ushered us to a small waiting area, a doctor walked into the room.

"I have good news and bad news," he told us. The good news was that Katie's heart rate was normal. The bad news was that, given the trauma she had suffered, it wasn't "normal to be normal." Also, Katie was not able to breathe on her own.

"I need to do more tests," the doctor explained. "Something is going on, and we just don't know what it is." We were relieved to hear that Katie's heart was still beating, fighting for life. The fact that she was still alive gave us some hope.

It wasn't long after that the chaplain moved us to another room. It was a quieter and more comfortable room, where nobody else was around. I knew then this meant something was going to be very bad.

And while Gary and Heidi still clung to hope, the doctor walked in and, with tears filling his eyes, confirmed our worst fears.

"She didn't make it."

We later learned that Katie's spinal cord had been instantly severed by the accident, which was why she couldn't breathe on her own. Technically dead, she was still on life support as we walked into ICU to see her. I couldn't help but think how peaceful and beautiful she looked even then, her cheeks still flush with color. It broke my heart.

The fact that Katie is gone is still pretty hard to accept. Even as I wrote this story, a part of me still clings to hope that this is just a bad dream—and somehow, Katie still lives. Of course, I know the truth all too well. But even though I know that Katie really is gone, this tendency to cling to hope reminds us of how precious and wonderful life really is, and how devastated we are when it is taken away.

My heart still aches for that nine-year-old beauty and the rest of her loving family who suffered such a terrible loss, especially Kelsie, Katie's big sister. The quieter of the two, Kelsie is always so perceptive and thoughtful, so mature for her age, and I can't imagine how a 12-year-old like her could handle this. That tragic day when we lost Katie still plays like slow motion in my mind's eye, and being a part of it has prompted a lot of soul-searching in my own life.

Perhaps you can relate to our family tragedy. If you have lived very long, it's likely that you have lost a close friend or family member. Perhaps you, like me, are still clinging to some measure of hope. You know that your loved one is gone, yet you just don't want to accept it.

Come, Let us Reason Together

On the surface, the tragic story told in this chapter is full of horrific imagery that naturally elicits a mountain of emotion. So it's natural to wonder, "Who can think reasonably when confronted with such a crisis?"

Yet it is when we come face to face with this human enemy—death—that reasonable thinking is most needed. If we would find answers to our questions about death we must reason with one another. To overcome confusion and despair, we must use common sense and look at it as objectively as humanly possible.

The topic of what happens when a person dies is an important one, deserving of careful study. While death is never an easy or fun matter to discuss, there is much to be gained. From my own personal experience, I know that as you explore what happens to those who die, where they go, and what they are feeling now, you will discover a sense of peace you have never known before.

If you would like to embark on a journey that will change your life, to have a Bible-based understanding on the topic of death, keep exploring the pages of this book—keep turning the pages.

Final Thought

In this world, terrible things happen—many things that we just cannot explain. Sometimes we even get bitter and close our hearts to the very things that can help us understand and cope better. Yet if we will by faith and hope open ourselves up to truth, however tough that seems to be, we will find peace.

2

Questions of Life and Death

There is nothing quite so tragic as making funeral arrangements for a child. It's a grief that only a world full of evil could know. As the saying goes, "No parent should have to bury their child." That might be a cliché, but it's powerfully true nonetheless.

I've witnessed grieving parents shaken to the core—choosing a coffin, buying a grave plot, and signing a contract—all so they could bury their loved one. It's the closest thing to torture I've seen, and no matter how I look at it, the process just doesn't make sense.

Yet as strange as it seemed to make those arrangements, the irony of laying a child to rest wasn't the thing that struck me most. Rather, what really got to me was that, despite the fact that our culture treats death as an endless mystery and uncertainty, everyone still thinks they know exactly what happened to the person who died. This was certainly the case with Katie.

"All her troubles are over now," were some of the well-intentioned words we heard. "Katie is in heaven with Jesus." At Katie's funeral, the pastor had her up in heaven, playing on a swing, looking down on us, and having an incredible time.

Now, I understand that the pastor's words were a comfort to many hearts, especially in the face of a terrible tragedy. Yet I couldn't help but wonder—how could Katie be so blissfully happy up there looking down on us—when we are so incredibly sad? While this might seem like a strange line of reasoning, you might also know how it is when people are in such a state of grief: your mind works so fast that thoughts tumble over themselves.

The more I thought about it, the more this whole idea confused me. If Katie truly was up in heaven watching us, as the pastor said, how could she be so filled with joy when her parents were grieving their hearts out? Katie loved her parents so very much; it seemed to me that the only way she could be so happy when they were so sad was if God took away part of her memory. Then perhaps she wouldn't know that those people she was watching, who were so overtaken with grief, were all her family and friends.

Of course, this line of thought brought up a new set of questions. If we go to heaven right after we die, do we then forget who we are? While this seems like the only way we could be so blissful when our loved ones are wrapped in grief, why would we then bother to spend our time in heaven watching people we don't even know? On the other hand, if we do retain our memories and identities when we get to heaven, what would Jesus have to do to distract us or make us have fun when people we love are crying over our casket?

Yet Katie's pastor seemed to suggest that Katie was still Katie, that she knew who she was and who we were, and that she was having a wonderful time. This just didn't make sense to me, however, and the more I listened to his and other comments, the more questions I had.

Another person suggested that Katie was now with her grandma. They were together, playing in heaven, and watching over us. Now I couldn't figure out how they could be even remotely happy in heaven while watching their loved ones suffer, not only at that moment, but into the future.

Still, the most powerful moment for me came when I stood over Katie's casket, looking down at her one last time. "If you're in heaven right now," I wondered, "why are you still here?"

Have you ever stopped to consider how confusing many of our comments and beliefs about the dead—however well-intentioned—are? If you've never considered it, what do you think about it now? Does it really make sense? It seems unlikely to me that I'm the only one who has ever wondered how our loved ones could be living so joyfully up in heaven while their family and friends are grieving and suffering on earth.

If your friends and relatives who have passed on are truly up in heaven watching you, what would they think if they saw you behaving badly? The thought alone can be somewhat unnerving. The idea that somebody in heaven might get to know us much better than they ever could on earth is really not a welcome concept. Even if you have nothing to hide, there are some areas of your life you'd prefer to keep private!

At Katie's funeral, the pastor's statement that she was in heaven got me thinking about others who might be less fortunate. If they don't go to heaven, do they go straight to hell? I don't know about you, but I've never been to a funeral where the pastor even remotely suggests that the person has gone to hell.

This in itself seems strange, because a lot of preachers aren't the least bit timid about saying that people who commit certain sins will go to hell when they die. "Such and such group will burn in the eternal lake of fire," they preach. Yet when someone from that class of people die, I never hear anything about burning at the funeral. Even if the person who died wasn't a Christian, pastors routinely suggest that they are in heaven. "They are in a better place now," they say.

So while in the churches it seems like there is a heaven to win and a hell to shun, at funerals it seems like there is only a heaven. Which brings up yet one more question. If the first stop after death is heaven regardless of how a person lived, does God transfer some people out of heaven, sending them on to hell at some later date? And if He does, how would we know?

Right after Katie's funeral, someone sent a message to her grieving parents and asked if they would like to know more about Katie's "new life" in heaven. The person claimed to be in some type of direct communication with their daughter, a paranormal getting messages straight from above.

But while the very thought of this person bothered me, the idea of what she said troubled me even more. And I wondered—if people in heaven can speak to you, can the residents of hell dial your number as well? Is there a reliable rulebook for who can and cannot visit you from the grave? How would we know that this medium was really talking to Katie? Did she want money for her services? How could we know that her intentions were pure? We didn't even know her.

If a friend of mine died and started talking to me, how could I be sure that he was calling from heaven? Would I simply have to believe whatever he said? The Bible says that even the devil can masquerade as an angel of light (2 Corinthians 11:14). If we can be visited by people from both heaven and hell, couldn't those from hell tempt you to do bad things just as surely as those who are watching from heaven might encourage you to do good things?

Ultimately, how can we know if someone has gone to heaven or hell? And what right do we have to make a comment on the matter—especially since we often don't have all the facts? For example, if a father who has been secretly abusing his children dies, would they want to know that he was looking down on them all the time from heaven, hoping the best for their lives?

Do you see the problems connected with the popular beliefs about what happens when a person dies? Do I make any sense? Without a doubt, there has to be some kind of truth about the situation, and I want to know that truth. Even if the truth were "nothing happens after death," at least I wouldn't have to wonder about it. At least when I heard differing opinions or ideas, I would know the facts. After all, who wants to feel confused every time they walk out of a funeral? Who wants these questions to plague, and continue to plague, them while they are grieving?

I needed answers, and needed them badly, but where would I turn to get them? How could I know for sure what happened to little Katie?

Final Thought

No matter what we go through or whatever pain that we might bear, let's reason together. The Bible tells us that God is not the author of confusion; rather, He is the way, the truth, and the life (John 14:6). If we search for Him with all our hearts, we will find Him and the answers to life's most perplexing questions (See Jeremiah 29:13).

3

Where Do
We Turn?

I sat next to two friends at the breakfast table one morning. One was an early riser, the other an evening person. The "night owl" had been getting out of bed early for six days straight, and I could tell he was on the verge of falling asleep any moment. At one point in our conversation, rubbing his tired eyes, he asked, "What day is it today?"

"Tuesday," I answered.

He shook his weary head in disbelief.

"It feels like Wednesday. Why is that?"

"It feels like Tuesday to me," piped up the wide-awake early riser.

This conversation, however mundane, has stuck with me because of the important principal it demonstrates. Both of my friends are intelligent people, familiar with the weekly calendar. Yet both had mentioned how they "felt" about the day. One felt it was Wednesday, and he was wrong. The other felt it was Tuesday, and he was right.

Based on this little story, it doesn't seem safe to rely on feelings to determine which day of the week it is. We need some sort of reference point, not intuition or feelings, to help us know whether it's Tuesday, Wednesday, or some other day. The fact that you distrust the sleepyhead and "feel" that he is unreliable doesn't automatically mean the early riser is right.

It seems to me that the only way to be sure of the day of the week is to research the facts. That might be as simple as looking at your watch, a calendar, or the internet. Indeed, the only way to know just about anything is by doing some form of research.

And that's the way I approached clearing up the confusion about whether my niece was up in heaven looking down on us—through research. That's how scientists try to answer their questions, and it seemed like the most logical approach to the questions I was pondering.

Many people believe that feelings are never wrong. In fact, many rely on those feelings to make important decisions. But as we've seen, even on the most trivial of matters, feelings can be quite misleading, even confusing. If someone can feel "wrong" about the day, might they not also be wrong when they say, "I feel like Jane is sitting right here next to me," or, "I feel like nothing happens when we die?"

Could the pastor have been wrong about Katie? My mind certainly entertained the possibility that he was wrong, even though most people believed that what he said was true. And it could very well be true, but the point is, how would I know?

There have been times in my life when I have "known" something was so right that there was simply no discussion about it. Yet in the end, when I looked at the facts, I found that I had been absolutely wrong.

This same principle is at work in the life of every human being. We all believe something. I believe something and you believe something. Even atheists believe something. But if those beliefs are based merely on hearsay, feelings, or intuition, there is the very real possibility that even our most cherished beliefs are wrong.

With this in mind, it's important for us to think about what we base our beliefs on. Think about it—what are your beliefs about death based on? Have you studied it out for yourself? If your beliefs are based on feelings, how might you determine what you believe? How can you know if your feelings are accurate? And if your feelings disagree with the feelings of others on the same subject, how can you know which "feelings" are right?

As mentioned in the preface, throughout this book, we're going to draw heavily from the commentary of one of Christianity's most influential and prolific writers. Her exposition on the truth regarding the dead and spirit world is the best source outside of the Bible you'll ever find. In order to make it clear which thoughts are drawn from her writings and which are my own, the adapted works will be printed in a different (Helvetica) font.

> **For Christians, the best information source for truth is the Bible. In other words, we should hold every belief we have up to the light of God's Word. If our beliefs or feelings, no matter how cherished, disagree with God's Word—it is because there is no light in them.**

The Bible a Safeguard

In the words of the prophet Isaiah, "To the law and to the testimony: if they speak not according to this word, it is because there is no light in them" (Isaiah 8:20).

Satan is using every tool in his arsenal to prevent people from learning about the Bible. He knows that the plain truths of the Bible reveal his deceptions. Every time there is a revival of God's work, the devil takes his level of activity to new heights. At this very moment, he is putting forth his utmost efforts in the final struggle against Christ and His followers.

The last great delusion is soon to open before us. The antichrist will soon perform his marvelous works right before our very eyes. So closely will the counterfeit resemble the true, it will be impossible to tell the difference except through the Holy Scriptures. Every testimony, every miracle, must be tested against the Bible.

Those who endeavor to obey all the commandments of God will be opposed and made fun of. They can stand only in God. In order to endure the trial before them, they will need to understand the will of God as revealed in His Word. Yet they can only truly honor God if they truly understand—and act in accordance with— His character, government, and purpose.

None but those who have fortified their minds with the truths of the Bible will stand through the last great conflict. To every soul will come the searching test: Shall I obey God rather than man? The decisive hour is even now at hand. Are our feet planted on the rock of God's immutable Word? Are we prepared to stand firm in defense of the commandments of God and the faith of Jesus? (See Revelation 14:12.)

When we feel confused or aren't sure what to believe, the Bible can clear things up and illuminate the way. "Thy word is a lamp unto my feet, and a light unto my path" (Psalms 119:105).

A Terrible Mistake

At the crucifixion of Jesus, the disciples of Christ made a terrible mistake. Jesus had explained to them how He must suffer for the sins of this world, and then be raised from the tomb. Angels of God had been sent to impress these thoughts into the disciples' minds, so that they would understand and be strengthened during the difficult days ahead.

Yet in spite of the clear explanation Jesus gave to the disciples about the terrible events about to transpire, the horrors of the crucifixion found them totally unprepared.

The disciples were more interested in victory over the Romans than a spiritual rule. The idea that Jesus, the center of all their hopes, might die a humiliating death rather than fulfill their dreams was more than they thought they could bear.

And so the words they needed so badly to remember were banished from their minds. When the time of trial came, it found them unprepared. The death of Jesus as fully destroyed their hopes as if He had not forewarned them!

History Repeated

Unfortunately, it's all too easy for us to make the same type of mistake today. God has told us many important things in the Bible. Bible prophecies open the future to us just as plainly as it was opened to the disciples by the words of Christ. Yet many have no more understanding of these important truths than if they had never been revealed. This is because Satan, our great enemy, is carefully sweeping away every impression that would open our minds to the truth.

Jesus had a good reason for calling Satan "the Father of Lies" (John 8:44). Satan is the enemy of truth, bent on using every possible device to prevent us from knowing and understanding our Bibles. For every Bible truth, Satan has a counterfeit so closely resembling the true that it is impossible to distinguish between them except through the Holy Scriptures.

This is why we must hold everything—even our long-standing

and cherished beliefs about death—up to the light of God's Word. We simply cannot rely upon feelings. If we are not careful, we have the same experience of disbelief that Jesus' disciples had in their hour of crisis. It is up to us to learn from their example, so that we will not be deceived in the closing hours of this earth's history.

Angels Flying Through Heaven

In the Bible, the word angel means "a messenger," or one who is sent from God (Luke 1:19). So when God sends warnings to earth so important that they are represented as proclaimed by holy angels flying in the midst of heaven (Revelation 14), He requires every person endowed with reasoning powers to heed the message. Yet the vast majority of people turn away their ears from hearing the truth because they would rather hear fables.

The apostle Paul foresaw this when he predicted that in the last days, "the time will come when they will not endure sound doctrine" (2 Timothy 4:3). Most people do not want to hear the truth, because it interferes with the desires of the sinful, world-loving heart. And Satan is oh so willing to supply the deceptions that they love!

But God will have a people on the earth who rely on the Bible, and the Bible only, as the rule of their life and basis for every belief. There are four substitutes striving to take the place of God's Word in our lives:

- the opinions of learned men
- the deductions of science
- the creeds and councils of churches, and
- the voice of the majority

Not one of these should be regarded as evidence for or against a point of truth. Realizing that the opinions of man are not reliable as a basis for religious faith, God's true followers will require a plain "Thus saith the Lord" before adopting any new doctrine or precept.

Yes, for Christians, the correct source of truth about anything is the Bible. Without the Bible, anyone can come along and tell you what they think, and you would have no way of knowing what is true or false. Think about it—if we trust what the Bible has to say about Jesus, shouldn't we also rely on what it says about other important matters, like what happens when we die? Indeed, because there is so much deception in this world from so many evil sources ready to lead us astray, the Bible should be the first and only thing we trust.

This is why, in my search for truth about Katie and others who have died, I knew that I had to stick to the Bible for answers. I could not rely on other peoples' opinions or dreams of the afterlife—no matter how beautiful they were or how convincingly they were presented.

Truth is based on facts, not emotion. It's not Wednesday because it feels that way; it's Wednesday because Tuesday just happened and Thursday is about to happen. Similarly, my beliefs about what happened to Katie and others who have "gone before" must be based on fact, not emotion. Fortunately, God has not left us without information. The Bible has plenty to say about both the spirit world and the dead.

If you would like to know what the Bible teaches about where the dead are now and where they are going—I invite you to continue turning the pages of this book. Because when you understand what God really does teach about these things, you really will have a peace that "passes all understanding" (Philippians 4:7).

Final Thought

We should never be upset when we find out we are wrong. To defend ourselves for the sake of ourselves is not only selfish but dangerous, especially when we convince others we are right when we really are wrong. Our goal should always be to find the truth no matter what our feelings are screaming in our ears. Remember, truth can always stand to be examined.

4

Why it Matters What You Believe About Death

If you're a natural skeptic like me, I urge you to keep reading for the following reason: No harm can come from hearing out all the pieces of data from which you can make an informed decision. If you are unsure about something you've read, keep reading, because the next few paragraphs might have the answer. Whatever you do, just keep reading. Get all the facts before you decide what is true and what is false.

"It really doesn't matter what you believe about the dead," my friend assured me. "As long as your beliefs are a comfort to you, and my beliefs are a comfort to me, that's what counts."

On the surface, this philosophy sounds pretty appealing. And it certainly is a popular one in this live and let live world. After all, why should you and I quibble over what happens when a person dies? Even if what I believe is biblically incorrect, why upset the apple cart? If my beliefs—no matter how erroneous—bring me some measure of comfort in the face of great loss, why not enjoy whatever happy thoughts I can muster and let the matter alone?

These are certainly valid questions, ones that deserve to be asked as we ponder the question of what happens to a person when he or she dies. Yet after careful study of the matter, I believe that what you believe about the dead really does matter.

The bottom line is, we cannot live a life that glorifies God apart from Bible truth. Since copies of the Bible are easily accessible, there is really no excuse for cherishing unbiblical opinions. Indeed, we dishonor God when we have His "guidebook for life" in our homes, but somehow don't bother to learn for ourselves what it says.

"It doesn't matter what you believe," is the popular teaching of the day. "It only matters if your life is right." Yet the life is molded by faith in truth or fables. Neglecting the light and truth that are within our reach is the same as rejecting it: We are choosing darkness rather than light.

"There is a way that seemeth right unto a man, but the end thereof are the ways of death" (Proverbs 16:25). When there is every opportunity to know the will of God, ignorance is no excuse for error or sin.

When a traveler comes to a fork in the road and ignores the directional road signs, sincerity will not save him. He may be very sincere, but he will be headed in the wrong direction nonetheless.

The same is true in your spiritual walk: The path you choose will lead you one way or the other. If you ignore or neglect to study the plain truths of God's Word, sincerity will not save you.

Our Personal Road Map

God gave us the gift of His Word so that we could become acquainted with His teachings and know personally what He requires of us. When the rich young ruler came to Jesus with the question, "What shall I do to inherit eternal life?" Jesus referred him to the Scriptures.

"What is written in the law?" were the words of the Savior. "How readest thou?" Ignorance will not release young or old, or release them from the punishment due for the transgression of God's law. God has placed a faithful presentation of His law in our hands, and He expects us to use it.

It is not enough to have good intentions. Good intentions will not save you. As the old saying goes, "The path to hell is paved with good intentions."

Doing what "you think is right" will also not save you. Doing what your pastor says is right is not enough. Your soul is at stake! You must search the Scriptures for yourself. No matter how strong your convictions are, no matter how confidently you feel that your pastor knows the truth, this should not be the foundation of your religion. In the Bible, God has given you a chart pointing out every landmark on the way to heaven. There is no need to guess at anything.

As a human being, created in the image of God, it is your first and highest duty to learn from the Bible what is truth. Then you must walk in the light and encourage others to follow your example. Study your Bible diligently, day by day. Weigh every thought, comparing Scripture with Scripture. With divine help, you can study and form opinions for yourself. Someday you—not your pastor or professor—will give an answer for yourself at the judgment throne of God. How imperative it is, then, that you know personally from the Bible what you believe, and why you believe it.

Fortified with God's Essential Word

If you neglect Bible study and prayer, you make yourself more susceptible to the temptations of Satan. In fact, they may seem irresistible. If God's Word isn't hidden in your heart, you won't be readily able to remember appropriate verses in your hour of need.

If you are taught as a child by Jesus, however, you can be sure that heavenly angels will surround you and, in your hour of necessity, help you remember the very truths you need. Thus "when the enemy shall come in like a flood, the Spirit of the Lord shall lift up a standard against him" (Isaiah 59:19).

Jesus promised that "the Comforter, the Holy Ghost, whom the Father will send in my name, He shall teach you all things, and bring all things to your remembrance, whatsoever I have said unto you" (John 14:26). But the teachings of Christ must previously have been stored in the mind in order for the Spirit of God to bring them to our remembrance in the time of peril. "Thy word have I hid in mine heart," said David, "that I might not sin against Thee" (Psalm 119:11).

Now Is the Time

We truly live in a momentous hour of this earth's history. Our own future destiny, and that of many others, depends on the course that we take. We need to be guided, as never before, by the Spirit of truth. Every follower of Jesus should be on their knees as never before, pleading, "Lord, what wilt Thou have me to do?"

We need to humble ourselves before the Lord. We need to fast and pray. We need to meditate on God's Word—especially on the scenes of God's judgment. And we need to seek a deep and living experience—as we have never had before—in the things of God. We have not a moment to lose. Events of vital importance are taking place around us. We are on Satan's enchanted ground.

We need to wake up—and realize that when the testing time shall come, those who have made God's Word their rule of life will be revealed. In summer, there isn't much difference between evergreens and other trees. But when the blasts of winter come and other trees are stripped of their foliage, the evergreens are still beautiful, vibrant, and green.

There might not be much outward difference between the false-hearted Christian and the true right at this moment, but the time is coming quickly when the difference will be very apparent. Let opposition arise, let bigotry and intolerance rear their ugly heads, let persecution be kindled, and the halfhearted and hypocritical will waver and yield the faith. The true Christian, however, will stand firm as a rock, his faith stronger, his hope brighter, than in the days of prosperity.

"Happy is the man that findeth wisdom" (Proverbs 3:13). "He shall be as a tree planted by the waters, and that spreadeth out her roots by the river, and shall not see when heat cometh, but her leaf shall be green; and shall not be careful in the year of drought, neither shall cease from yielding fruit" (Jeremiah 17:8).

Final Thought

Whenever we stray from God's Word, even just a little bit, we eventually find ourselves in big trouble. (Believe me, I'm an expert on the matter.) I know that accepting the smallest error will often lead us into accepting even greater errors that lead us down a slippery slope to unbelief.

However, if we learn to trust His Word as a whole, no matter how much or how passionately others object, we will find tremendous peace within that no storm can batter down.

And think about this . . . if it doesn't really matter what you believe about death, why does God even bother mentioning it in His Word? Might He have used that space for something that will matter in the end? The keys of life are found in the Bible. In my opinion, anything in there is in there for a very good reason. What do you think?

5

Five Steps to Understanding the Bible

It goes without saying that before you can understand what the Bible says about death, you must first have some idea of how to study your Bible. Not that studying the Bible is so difficult, but there is a right and wrong way to go about it. Following are five steps that have been very important to me as I opened God's Word on the important topic of death and dying.

Step #1: Start with a Childlike Spirit

The key to understanding the Bible is to have the meekness and submission of a little child. While studying the deep things of God certainly requires all the powers of our minds, we don't have to be doctors or philosophers to understand the Bible. The research methods of science and philosophy simply won't work here, and neither will the self-confident spirit of many intellectuals.

We need a prayerful, childlike dependence on God if we would understand the Bible. A sincere desire to learn God's will plus a humble and teachable spirit are also prerequisites for learning at the feet of Jesus. Having a childlike spirit is important. If we neglect to make the necessary attitude adjustments before opening God's Word, evil angels will so blind and harden our hearts that we will not be impressed by the truth.

Step #2: Keep it Simple

Many of the truths that the Bible reveals most plainly have been plunged into doubt and darkness by those who call themselves Bible scholars. Pretending to have great wisdom, they teach that the Bible has secret and mystical spiritual meanings that are hard to understand. These men are false teachers, and they are the ones Jesus was addressing when He said, "Ye know not the Scriptures, nor the power of God" (Mark 12:24).

Many portions of Scripture that have been pronounced a mystery by Bible scholars, or are passed over as not important, are full of comfort and instruction to humble learners in the school of Christ.

One reason why many theologians have such a murky understanding of God's Word is that they close their eyes to truths they don't wish to practice. Understanding the Bible truth doesn't take a Master of Divinity. What is needed is a singleness of purpose and an earnest longing after righteousness.

Unless a symbol or figure is employed by the Bible, God's Word should be explained according to its obvious meaning. "If any man will do His will, he shall know of the doctrine," was the promise of Christ (John 7:17). If people would take the Bible simply—as it reads—with no false teachers to mislead or confuse their minds, a work would be accomplished that would make angels glad and thousands upon thousands who are now wandering in error would be led into the fold of Christ.

Step #3: Always Pray First

The Bible should never be studied without prayer. Only the Holy Spirit can help us understand the importance of things that are easily understood. The Holy Spirit can also prevent us from twisting truths that are difficult to comprehend.

As you open the Scriptures, God will send angels to your side. They will prepare your heart and help you to understand His Word so that you will be charmed by its beauty, admonished by its warnings, or animated and strengthened by its promises. As you delve deeper into God's Word, the psalmist's petition should be your own: "Open Thou mine eyes, that I may behold wondrous things out of Thy law" (Psalm 119:18).

Step #4: Banish Skeptical Thoughts

If heaven is your goal, be on your guard against skepticism. It's nearly impossible to live in this world without running into the insinuations of doubt, sarcasm, and infidelity. It seems that Satan, who is a master at adaptation, has something for everyone. Christians who don't read well are met with a sneer, while the educated are met with scientific objections and philosophical reasoning. Both strategies are meant to excite distrust in God's Holy Word.

Even young people, who early in their lives should spend more time studying and less time philosophizing, think nothing of pouring contempt on the fundamental principles of Christianity. And their infidelity, shallow as it is, has an influence. Many are thus led to joke about the faith of their fathers and insult the Spirit of grace (Hebrews 10:29).

Do not be fooled, however. It is a dangerous thing to trust in boastful human reason. All who imagine that they can explain divine mysteries and arrive at truth without God's help are really deceived and entangled in the snares of Satan.

Step #5: Study Things Out for Yourself

In the days of Jesus, the priests and rulers exercised too much authority over the religious life of the people. Looking down through the centuries, Jesus saw that this practice of giving the teachings of men precedence over the plain Word of God would happen over and over again.

When Jesus denounced the scribes and Pharisees, warning the people not to follow the "blind leading the blind," He wasn't just talking to the people of His day. The words of Christ were placed on record as an admonition to future generations.

Though the Reformation made the Bible available to all, many today are not searching its pages as they should. Somehow they have been deluded into thinking that the Bible must be explained. Taught to accept Bible teachings only as interpreted by the church, they dare not receive anything—no matter how plainly revealed by Scripture—that is contrary to the established teaching or creed of their church.

The Bible is full of warnings against false teachers, yet many seem ready to commit the keeping of their souls to the clergy. Today there are thousands of Christians who can give no other reason for their points of faith than that they were thus taught by their leaders. They pass by the words of Jesus almost unnoticed and place implicit confidence in the words of their pastors.

But are pastors infallible? Is it safe to trust our salvation to their hands—unless we have tested their words against God's

Word and know they are truly light bearers? Too many of us lack the moral courage to step outside of the beaten path. And so we follow in the steps of learned men, and by our reluctance to investigate the teachings of the Bible for ourselves, become hopelessly fastened in the chains of error.

We may see that the truth for this time is plainly taught in the Bible. We may feel the power of the Holy Spirit attending the reading of God's Word. Yet somehow we allow the teachings of learned men to turn us from the light. Though reason and conscience are convinced, such deluded souls dare not think differently from their minister. And thus their individual judgment and eternal interests are sacrificed to the unbelief, pride, and prejudice of another.

Satan is always trying to get us to follow human leaders in place of God. He would much rather that we look to bishops, pastors, professors, and prelates as our guides, than have us search the Scriptures for ourselves. The devil is smart enough to know that when we blindly follow our leaders, we save him a lot of work. He is an expert at delegating. All he has to do then is deceive the leaders, who will influence their followers to do his satanic bidding.

In Jesus' day, the common people heard Him gladly. It was the priests and rulers—the pastors, so to speak—who condemned and tried to repudiate His teachings. Though they were baffled in their efforts, and convicted of both His wisdom and divinity, still they stiffened their prejudice against Him. In their proud efforts to avoid becoming His disciples, they rejected the clearest evidences that Jesus was indeed the Messiah.

The people of Jesus' day had been taught to respect and reverence their rulers, to bow without question to their spiritual authority.

"How is it," they wanted to know, "that our learned and pious men do not believe in Jesus? If Jesus were really the Messiah, wouldn't our religious leaders be the first to know and accept Him?"

It was the influence of these revered Jewish leaders—the ones who rejected Christ—that led the Jews as a nation to reject the Messiah. Unfortunately, the same spirit that motivated the priests and rulers is still manifested by many who make a high profession of piety. These false shepherds rely on their feelings rather than a plain "Thus saith the Lord." Pointing to their own numbers, wealth, and popularity as tokens of God's affection, they look with contempt on those who would study the Bible simply and take God at His Word.

Satan, working through other people, has numerous ways to influence and bind his captives. He secures multitudes to himself by attaching them by the silken cords of affection to those who are enemies of the cross of Christ. Whether this attachment is parental, filial, marital, or social, the effect is the same. The opposers of truth exert their power to control the conscience, and the souls held under their sway lack the courage or independence to obey their own convictions of duty.

Final Thought

In all my studies of the Bible, I've learned that if we come to Jesus with a heart that is open and willing to know the truth, He will lead us step by step until the truth is as plain as day. However, when we are uncertain about truth, we must ask God to show us His understanding, and not the one we would rather have because it sounds better.

And He will do this if we show perseverance and patience. You'll also see that it won't happen by one text, but by "every word that proceeds out of the mouth of God." God will lead you so that the truth unfolds before you like a beautiful flower. Indeed, you will not believe the blessings you will gain from this practical but often unused principle.

6

Are There Spirits Among Us?

Of all the stories about UFOs, none has so arrested the popular imagination as the case of Betty and Barney Hill. First publicized in October 1965 by the *Boston Traveler,* the Hill story achieved one of the highest levels of public recognition of any UFO report. Today, more than 40 years later, it continues to generate intense curiosity.

Barney and his wife Betty had been suffering horrible lifelike nightmares for three years. One of their friends suggested that they seek hypnotherapy to discover the source behind their terror-filled dreams.

Through hypnotic regression, the pair was apparently able to remember that while vacationing on September 19, 1961, they spotted a bright light following them from the sky. As the story goes, Barney climbed out of the car to take a closer look at the now descending unidentified flying object. To his amazement, strange beings were staring at him from the windows!

When the terrified Barney tried to run away, both he and his wife were abducted by gray colored monsters. Forced to board an alien spacecraft, they were reportedly subjected to a frightening array of torturous experiments.

This incident was the first alien abduction story to receive broad media publicity. A successful made for television movie was even produced about it. However, not much physical evidence from the event, if any, has ever been produced. Claims were made that Betty, who was unfamiliar with astronomy, was able to chart two unknown stars before they were discovered. In the end, however, this turned out to be pure speculation.

And thus it has always been with alien abductions and other close encounters: lots of imaginative stories with little physical evidence to back them. Yet so many countries, from Australia to Iran, have UFO and abduction stories streaming out of them. Is it thus possible that some kind of extraterrestrial beings, far different from humans, visit the earth and interact with us?

In a very meaningful way, the answer to this question will help us open up the door to understanding what happened to Katie when she died. If we can understand one part of the spiritual world, maybe it will help us understand more about the afterlife.

What Do We Know About the Spirit World?

The Bible plainly teaches that there is both a visible and invisible world. Stories involving both heavenly angels and demonic powers are significant in the Bible, inseparably woven through the fabric of human history.

We know that angels existed before the creation of man, because when the foundations of the earth were laid, "the morning stars sang together, and all the sons of God shouted for joy" (Job 38:7).

After the fall of man, angels were sent to guard the tree of life. The Bible also tells us that by nature, angels are superior to man, for man was made "a little lower than the angels" (Psalm 8:5).

We know from the Bible that there are thousands and probably millions of angels. We can also safely deduce that angels are very powerful and glorious beings that are involved in both God's government and His plans for saving us.

If you doubt these things, consider the following verses. "The Lord hath prepared His throne in the heavens; and His kingdom ruleth over all" (Psalm 103:19). "I heard the voice of many angels round about the throne" (Revelation 5:11). In the presence chamber of the King of Kings are "angels that excel in strength," "ministers of His, that do His pleasure," "hearkening unto the voice of His Word."

In his vision, the prophet Daniel saw "ten thousand times ten thousand, and thousands of thousands" of heavenly beings (Daniel 7:10). The apostle Paul said the angels are an "innumerable company" (Hebrews 12:22). Their glory is so dazzling and their flight so swift that, when sent forth as God's messengers, they have "the appearance of a flash of lightning" (Ezekiel 1:14). The angel that appeared at the Savior's tomb had a countenance "like lightning, and his raiment white as snow" (Matthew 28:3). The keepers of the grave shook in fear when they saw him, and "became as dead men" (Matthew 28:4).

God sent His mightiest angel to deal with Sennacherib, a haughty Assyrian king. Sennacherib had committed the grievous crime of openly blaspheming God. In addition, he was threatening to destroy God's people, Israel. And so "it came to pass in the night, that the angel of the Lord went out, and smote in the camp of the Assyrians an hundred fourscore and five thousand" (2 Kings 19:35). There were "cut off all the mighty men of valor, and the leaders and captains" from the army of Sennacherib. "So he returned with shame of face to his own land" (2 Chronicles 32:21).

The problem with extraterrestrials visiting the earth is the same problem humans will have visiting other planets— space and time. Without extreme faster-than-light technology, it would take ages for aliens to travel to the earth from the closest planet outside our solar system. Not only would they need time to gain scientific knowledge and invent and build highly sophisticated spacecraft, they would have had to leave hundreds of thousands of years ago just to get here today. Yet this by-numbers science hasn't stopped 50 percent of the public from believing that aliens have visited the earth making crop circles, mutilating cattle, and abducting people. Still, when you add the beliefs of a large percentage of the population to the biblical accounts, it seems likely that extraterrestrial beings do indeed visit this planet.

The Work of Good Angels

The Bible certainly includes many accounts of good angels being sent on missions of mercy to the children of God. Good angels were sent to:

- Abraham, with promises of blessing
- the gates of Sodom, to rescue righteous Lot from its fiery doom
- Elijah, as he was about to perish from weariness and hunger in the desert
- Elisha, with chariots and horses of fire surrounding the little town in which he was shut in by his foes
- Daniel, while he was seeking divine wisdom in the court of a heathen king, or abandoned to become the lions' prey
- Peter, to rescue him from the death sentence in Herod's dungeon and once again to dispatch him with the message of salvation to a Gentile stranger,
- prisoners at Philippi
- Paul and his companions in the night of tempest on the sea
- Cornelius, to open his mind to receive the gospel

As you may have guessed, this list of angel appearances described in the Bible is far from complete. The point is, however, that holy angels have ministered to God's people in all ages, and they continue to minister today.

A guardian angel is appointed to every follower of Christ. These heavenly watchers shield the righteous from the power of the wicked one. Satan himself recognized this fact when he said, "Doth Job fear God for nought? Hast not Thou made an hedge about him, and about his house, and about all that he hath on every side?" (Job 1:9, 10).

David describes the protection of heavenly angels around God's people in Psalm 34:7: "The angel of the Lord encampeth round about them that fear Him, and delivereth them."

Then there were the words of Jesus who, while lifting a little child upon his knee, said that we should "Take heed that ye despise not one of these little ones; for I say unto you, That in heaven their angels do always behold the face of My Father" (Matthew 18:10). In other words, the angels appointed to minister to God's children—whether large or small—have access to God's presence at all times.

What a comfort to God's people, as they are exposed to the deceptive power and unsleeping malice of the prince of darkness, to know that God's powerful angels are always by their side. Yet while there is no need to fear the forces of evil, the very fact that we are assured of protection against them confirms that they do exist. For while God is extremely powerful and has given his children promises of grace and protection, there are also mighty agencies of evil to be met. As much as we wish they didn't exist, the evil angels of Satan are numerous, determined, and untiring. Their malignity and power cannot be ignored, for if we would do battle with the enemy, we must be aware of his presence.

Final Thought

I don't know about alien abductions, because the proof is so weak, but I do know that the Bible is full of stories of incredible beings called angels.

God has given us a great blessing by sharing the good news of His angels that are sent to help us when we are in need. Indeed, all around you are angels whose only purpose is to keep you from danger and evil. It's a comfort to me to know that these spirits are among us every moment of every day.

Yet the danger is when we walk away from these protective spirits by allowing evil into our lives and neglecting God's Word. There is a war between good and evil going on right now on the other side of the spiritual veil, but we have nothing to fear if we stay close to God and make it possible for His angels to intervene in our behalf.

7

The Truth about
Demons

F ace it, Morneau, you're not your own master. I wish you were,
but you're not. The spirits own you in your entirety, and the
sooner you acknowledge that . . . the better off you'll be."
Roland began pacing the floor, wringing his hands. "What I'm about to
say to you I'd rather tell my enemies, instead of a longtime friend."

By then Roland was perspiring profusely, although it wasn't
warm in the room. "Your days are numbered—along with those of
the young couple responsible for leading you away from the master.
Come with me to see the high priest right now. He will restore you
to the spirits' favor, and all will be well. This way no one gets hurt."
Roland again had to pause for a couple of seconds to use his handker-
chief.

"One thing in particular the high priest wants you to realize—no
one has ever gotten out of our secret society alive. The spirits brought
you and me into it, we're to be in subjection to them, not they to us."

So goes the story of the late Roger Morneau, a man who had
turned away from God until he hated him. When a friend invited Roger
to join in demon worship, Roger was all too willing.

When Morneau finally discovered the good news of a loving
God and wanted to break away from demon worship, he ran into some
major complications. Namely, the demons Morneau had formerly
worshiped didn't want to let him go. To say they threatened him would
be an understatement.

Morneau's story of divine rescue from the world of Satanism is
terrifying, to say the least. Who were these "masters" who first ruled,
and then threatened, Roger Morneau? When we think of angels, we
often think of "good angels"—those who protect us or are sent to help

in time of need. The Bible makes it clear, however, that evil angels or spirits are just as real as their heavenly counterparts.

These "bad angels" actually lived in heaven at one time. Created sinless, they were just as powerful and glorious as the angels that now encircle God's throne.

Once they chose a downward path, however, these angels spiraled quickly downward on the slippery slope of depravity. When they realized how Satan had deceived them into rebelling against God, they became incredibly angry and vengeful. Having lost a lot of good things through a string of bad choices, they now find their only pleasure—and a most wretched one at that—in wreaking havoc on earth.

They are united with Satan in his rebellion against God and hatred toward man. Their entire unhappy existence now centers around two diabolical themes: thwarting God's plans and destroying humans. Satan has the full cooperation of evil angels in his war against God's government, and they are really quite organized.

The Bible tells us that there are different "orders" of evil angels. Perhaps, like the army, they have generals, corporals, captains, and so on. The Bible also tells us that evil angels have a system of organization or government, that they are very intelligent, and equally dishonest. We also know from the Bible that they are full of malice toward God and man.

Although the Old Testament occasionally mentions the existence and working of evil angels, it was during New Testament times that these demons manifested their power in the most striking way. Jesus came to earth with a plan to save fallen man, but unfortunately, Satan was equally determined to have his way.

At that point in the history of the world, Satan had succeeded in establishing idol worship in every country except Palestine. And so God sent Jesus, His only son, to the only people who were still resisting Satan's temptations. His mission: to shed the light of heaven upon its people.

It was an epic battle between two rival powers, each claiming supremacy. On the one hand, Jesus stretched out His arms of love, inviting all who would to find pardon and peace in Him. Satan and his angels understood fully that if Christ's mission was successful, their evil rule would come to a screeching halt. And so we find Satan in the time of Jesus, raging like a caged lion—defiantly exhibiting his power over the bodies and souls of men.

The New Testament is clear about demon possession. It is a Bible based fact that men and women can and do become devil possessed. Demon possessed individuals in the Bible were suffering from something supernatural, something much greater than mental illness. When He confronted these demons, Jesus knew exactly who He was dealing with. This is why, on more than one occasion, He rebuked the demons directly.

What we do know about alien beings is that according to the Bible, angels and demons are part of another plane of existence who can move to and fro with ease according to their purposes. The Bible also makes it clear that they have continuing, if not always regular, contact with human beings. In some cases, this activity is on our behalf; in other cases, it's dangerous and deadly. "For we wrestle not against flesh and blood, but against principalities, against powers, against the rulers of the darkness of this world, against spiritual wickedness in high places" (Ephesians 6:12).

What Powers Do Evil Angels Have?

A striking example of the number, power, and depths of hate to which evil angels will sink to—as well as the infinite power and mercy of Jesus—is given in the Bible story about the demon possessed men of Gadara.

These maniacs, who the Bible describes as wretched, writhing, and foaming at the mouth, behaved violently toward their own bodies and endangered all who approached them. Their bleeding, disfigured bodies were an amazing testimony to the power gripping their souls, and more often than not, the air was filled with their screams.

One of the demons controlling the sufferers declared, "My name is Legion: for we are many" (Mark 5:9). In the Roman army, a legion consisted of three to five thousand men. Satan's hosts also are marshaled in companies, and the single company to which these demons belonged numbered no less than a legion.

Even a legion of evil spirits was no match for the mighty voice of Jesus, however. At our Savior's command, the demons had no choice but to leave their victims. The two men then underwent an immediate and remarkable transformation. As soon as the demons left them, they sat calmly at the feet of Jesus. The wild look in their eyes had vanished, the last scream had left their lips. Now they were gentle, subdued, and intelligent.

The displaced demons apparently needed someplace else to go, or at least thought they did. So Jesus permitted them to sweep a herd of pigs into the sea.

This was a great financial loss to the farmers of Gadara, a loss that they felt far outweighed any blessings brought by Jesus. And so they begged Him to leave.

This was the result for which Satan had been hoping. By blaming Jesus for the loss of the swine, Satan hoped to prejudice the people and prevent them from hearing the message they needed so badly.

Jesus had several purposes in allowing the swine to plunge into the sea. By allowing the evil spirits to destroy the herd, God rebuked those who were raising these unclean beasts for the sake of gain. Actually, if Christ had not intervened, the farmer's loss would have been much worse. The demons would gladly have plunged not only the swine, but their keepers and owners into the frothing sea.

The preservation of the herdsmen and their employers was nothing short of a miracle, an example of God's power and mercy. Tragic as this event may seem for the animals involved, God permitted it to take place that the disciples might witness the cruel power of Satan upon both man and beast.

Jesus wanted His followers to be aware of the incredible evil their enemy was capable of, so they wouldn't be tricked or overcome by Satan's snares. Jesus also wanted to break the people of Gadara away from the slavery of materialism, to set an entire region of captives free. And so, though Jesus Himself left the town at the request of the people, the men He had so marvelously delivered remained behind to declare the mercy of their Benefactor.

Other instances of a similar nature are recorded in the Scriptures:

- The daughter of the Syrophoenician woman was grievously vexed with a devil, whom Jesus cast out by His Word (Mark 7:26-30).
- Matthew records the story of "one possessed with a devil, blind, and dumb" (Matthew 12:22).
- Mark recounts the story of a youth who had a dumb spirit, which "cast him into the fire, and into the waters, to destroy him" (Mark 9:17-27).
- Luke tells the story of a maniac who, tormented by "a spirit of an unclean devil," disturbed the Sabbath quiet of the synagogue at Capernaum (Luke 4:33-36).

All of the above were healed by a compassionate Savior. In nearly every instance, Jesus addressed the demon as an intelligent entity, commanding him to come out of his victim and to torment him no more. The worshipers at Capernaum, beholding His mighty power, "were all amazed, and spake among themselves, saying, What a word is this! for with authority and power He commandeth the unclean spirits, and they come out" (Luke 4:36).

Final Thought

Much of the world would laugh at the things learned in this chapter—but by doing so they are also laughing at the direct teachings of God. Now that you know about angels and demons from the Bible, you have a broader scope of truth that you can put to good use when temptation and lies come your way. Those who are laughing are at an awful disadvantage.

In the battle between good and evil, good and evil angels are doing all they can to deliver you. The good angels want to deliver you from evil, and the evil angels want to deliver you into the hands of evil. God's angels will only use reason and love to direct our actions, while evil angels will use deceits to get you to sin. Who really has your best interests in mind? Should you trust those who would lie to you, or those who would tell you the truth no matter how hard that truth might sound?

Ultimately, you and I have the final say about who wins. God gave us free will to choose who we'll follow. Let's choose the good.

8

Dangers of Dabbling
with Demons

If you listen to actress Shirley MacLaine's account of her past lives, she's just about done it all. According to MacLaine, she's been an Indian princess, peg-legged pirate, and a man from Atlantis. Perhaps her most intriguing story is how she was Charlemagne's mystical lover.

In her current life, MacLaine has become one of the world's foremost advocates of the New Age and spiritualism. By her own account, she was targeted, observed, and followed by unseen entities that watched her every move. The title of her best-selling book is a take off on the key phrase she says the spirits used to get her attention: "to get the fruit of the tree, you must go out on a limb."

MacLaine makes no bones about her interest in contacting the dead. She claims that actor Peter Sellers contacted her after his death. In 1983, when Paramount Pictures was attempting to notify MacLaine of an Oscar nomination, they searched the world over before finally locating MacLaine in Egypt, where she had been sleeping in the burial room of an Egyptian pyramid.

For all her eccentricities, MacLaine's popularity as a spiritual guide is nothing short of astounding. When she embarked on a seminar series in the late 1980s, she sold out reception halls across the country. MacLaine, whose religion includes heavy doses of spiritualism and UFOs, is now focusing her attention on teaching others what she has learned from the spirit world . . .

Although many Bible stories paint demon-possessed individuals as great sufferers, there are exceptions to this rule. The Bible gives several examples of people who, for the sake of obtaining supernatural power, actually welcomed satanic influences.

Simon Magus, Elymas the sorcerer, and the young lady who followed Paul and Silas at Philippi appear to be in this class of people who cooperate, rather than conflict, with evil angels.

Regardless of the claims that such individuals make about their levels of enlightenment and "higher consciousness," they are tampering with a very dangerous force. By attempting to contact the dead, they are also going against the direct and ample warnings of Scripture.

Many of those who claim to communicate with the dead deny that they are in contact with Satan and his angels. Some even deny that a devil exists at all. This plays right into Satan's hands, giving him and his angels an almost incalculable advantage. After all, how can poor mortals be on their guard against someone they don't even think exists?

Satan is more than happy to promote the idea that he doesn't exist. He loves to conceal himself and his manner of working. The last thing Satan wants is for people to become acquainted with his schemes and devices. In fact, such a disclosure would be his worst nightmare.

As we approach the end of time, Satan is working furiously to deceive and destroy. The Bible says that the devil will go about as a roaring lion, seeking whom he may devour. Many hapless victims who think they are listening to the dictates of their own "inner wisdom" are actually listening not to their inner selves—but to the suggestions of Satan himself.

According to some polls, nearly 75 percent of people on the earth believe in the existence of angels and demons—so the matter is hardly controversial. Judaism, Islam, and Catholic and Protestant Christianity all believe in the existence of angels and demons working for or against God's will.

The Devil Is in the Disguise

Satan is the father of lies, the master of disguise. Because he doesn't want anyone to know his real character and purpose, he loves it when people think he is nothing more than a joke. When artists paint him as ludicrous and loathsome, when cartoonists portray him as misshapen and beastly, the devil nearly bursts with satanic glee.

"Let those who think they are intelligent and well-informed laugh," sneers the devil, "I will have the last laugh." The battle is real, the devil is real, and your very life is at stake. But he doesn't want you to know it.

The fact that so many people wonder if the devil even exists is a testimony to his success at masking himself so well. Satan is very adept at getting even Christians to believe theories that directly contradict the plainest statements of Scripture.

Jesus knew that Satan can readily control the minds of those who are unconscious of his influence. That's why the Word of God gives us so many examples of Satan's diabolical work. By unveiling the workings of Satan, Jesus tried to place us on our guard against his assaults.

How to Avoid Deceit

Unless you live in an incredibly safe neighborhood, it's likely that you lock your door when you leave the house. You may even have a high-tech burglar alarm, motion detector, or other security devices installed in your home. Yet in spite of the care we take in securing our homes from thieves and other dangers, we seldom think twice about evil angels who are constantly seeking access into our lives.

Yet these evil angels would, if permitted, distract our minds, torment our bodies, destroy our possessions, and quite generally decimate our lives. Their only delight is in wreaking misery and destruction, and they are quite good at that.

Without Christ, we are helpless against evil angels. We certainly have no strength of our own. As a result, those who resist the help that is only available in Jesus are on very dangerous ground. Satan is free to manipulate them, as they have no power to resist him.

If it weren't for the superior power of Jesus, the power and malice of Satan would be truly alarming. Fortunately for the Christian, there is shelter and deliverance in Christ.

Those who follow Christ are safe under the shadow of His

wings. Angels that excel in strength are sent from heaven to protect them, and the wicked one cannot break through the guard that God has stationed about His people.

Final Thought

We often get caught up in making decisions purely by our emotions, without checking up on all the facts. So when something feels or looks good to us, we usually accept it.

Think about drug and alcohol addiction . . . our feelings like it because they make us feel good. I used to drink all the time, so I should know something about it. But I also know the facts—drugs and alcohol often cause us to do evil, and worse, they can kill.

Satan and his demons love it when they get us to do evil, especially when it harms ourselves. They don't care about you, and will do anything to make you commit even the "smallest" kinds of evil. Remember, 90 percent good and 10 percent bad is still very much bad. By accepting a little bad, we open ourselves up to much worse.

Shirley MacLaine opened herself up to one past life, and now she is utterly mired in error. Don't let evil deceive you like that. Make the Bible your rule of life and stay away from false doctrines and evil spirits.

9

When Angels
Went to War

On November 18, 1973, Betty Eadie died from complications due to routine surgery. When she somehow revived nine minutes later, she had an incredible story to tell.

While clinically dead, Betty's soul allegedly traveled to heaven. Beyond the pearly gates, she met angels and other spirits with fantastic knowledge to impart. For example, she contends that:

- Humans were with God in the beginning and helped Him create the earth;
- Eve didn't "sin," but rather started an "initiative" that made it possible for mankind to have children;
- We are inherently divine;
- Spirits from the other side will help us learn the lessons of life, and even aid in our progress;
- Death is a spiritual "rebirth," our "transition" to another state of being.

Betty Eadie achieved fame and fortune with a popular book describing her experience. *Embraced by the Light* was widely read in Christian circles, and so well accepted that it remained number one on the New York Times Bestseller list for over a year!

According to the *Dallas Morning News,* the book's greatest appeal "stems from the description of eternal life, a comforting notion for people who have survived a loved one or for those pondering their own fate."

What can we learn from Betty Eadie and her near-death experience (NDE)? The obvious is that near-death experiences tend to alter one's world view. Raymond Moody, an expert in the field of NDEs, has said that those who experience a near-death episode "emerge with an appreciation of religion that is different from the narrowly defined one established by most churches. They come to realize through this experience that religion is not a matter of one 'right' group versus several 'wrong' groups. People who undergo an NDE come out of it saying that religion concerns your ability to love—not doctrine and denominations. In short, they think that God is a much more magnanimous being than they previously thought, and that denominations don't count." This certainly was the case with Betty Eadie.

Betty Eadie is certainly not alone in her beliefs about spirit beings and the afterlife, and as our family grieved over the loss of Katie, I couldn't help but think about what this famous writer said about death. Did Katie experience something like Betty Eadie did? Is Katie traveling the heavens now, meeting with angels and other "helpful spirits?"

Betty Eadie is a professed, devoted Christian. If life happened after death, might she know the truth about the afterlife from her near-death experience? If so, how might we know it was accurate? If not, how could we be sure? Can what she learned about the history of the universe and the spirit world give us further insight into what happens when we die?

> **One reason why Betty Eadie's book topped the bestseller list for so long is because it proposed answers to peoples' deepest questions and, despite the fact that the answers were not particularly biblical, gave answers that people wanted to hear. They see wars like the one in Iraq, they see a tsunami that killed upwards of a quarter of a million people, they see starvation and AIDS and biological weapons and global warming and they wonder—if God is so good and kind, why does all this evil exist? If God truly is love and has such infinite power, why does He not use His power to stop all this pain?**

To better answer this question, we need to go back to the beginning—not of this world—but of angels and sin. We need to know why there are evil angels, and what they are doing to make truth more difficult to come by. It's also important to know why things went wrong and why we find ourselves in such a state of confusion.

How Did This All Begin

To many minds, the origin of sin and the reason for its existence are a source of great perplexity. People see the work of evil, with its terrible results of woe and desolation. This is a mystery for which many find no explanation. Troubled by uncertainty and doubt, they become blinded to truths plainly revealed in God's Word.

In their search for truth, some begin looking into things that God has never revealed. Then, finding no answer to their questions, they doubt and reject the words of truth in the Bible.

Tradition and misinterpretation obscure the truth for others in search of answers about the character of God, nature of His government, and manner of dealing with sin.

Even the best and brightest of men can't give a full explanation of the origin of sin, let alone a reason for its existence. There are simply some things that God has, in His great mercy, chosen not to reveal.

Despite the fact that unanswered questions remain, however, God has given us enough information about the origin and the final disposition of sin to allow us to understand His justice and benevolence in all His dealings with evil.

Nothing is more plainly taught in Scripture than that God was in no way responsible for the entrance of sin; that there was no arbitrary withdrawal of divine grace, no deficiency in the divine government, providing a reason for Satan's rebellion. Sin is an intruder for whose presence no reason can be given. It is mysterious, unaccountable; to excuse it is to defend it.

If an excuse could be found for sin, or a reason for its existence, it would cease to be sin. Our only definition of sin is that given in the Word of God: it is "the transgression of the law" (1 John 3:4); it is a principle at war with the great law of love that undergirds God's government.

What Was It Like in the Beginning?

Before the entrance of evil, peace and joy flowed throughout the universe. All was in perfect harmony with the Creator's will.

Love for God was supreme, love for one another impartial. Christ the Word, the Only Begotten of God, was one with the eternal Father—one in nature, in character, and in purpose—the only being in the universe who could enter into all the counsels and purposes of God.

God worked through Jesus to create all the heavenly beings. "By Him were all things created, that are in heaven . . . whether they be thrones, or dominions, or principalities, or powers" (Colossians 1:16); and to Christ, equally with the Father, all heaven gave allegiance [Philippians 2:1-8].

Because the law of love is the foundation God's government [Psalm 89:14; 85:10], the happiness of all created beings depended upon their obedience to that law [Matthew 5:1-12].

God wants all of His creatures to serve Him out of love—an intelligent love that springs from a true appreciation of His character. God takes no pleasure in a forced allegiance. He gives freedom of choice to everyone, in hopes that they will serve Him out of love, voluntarily and for the right reasons.

But there was one who chose to pervert this freedom. Amazingly enough, sin originated with the angel who, next to Christ, stood the very closest to God. Before his fall, Lucifer was holy and undefiled, first of the covering cherubs, the most honored of God who stood highest in power among all the inhabitants of heaven.

"Thus saith the Lord God; Thou sealest up the sum, full of wisdom, and perfect in beauty. Thou hast been in Eden the garden of God; every precious stone was thy covering. . . . Thou art the anointed cherub that covereth; and I have set thee so: thou wast upon the holy mountain of God; thou hast walked up and down in the midst of the stones of fire. Thou wast perfect in thy ways from the day that thou wast created, till iniquity was found in thee" (Ezekiel 28:12-15).

Lucifer might have remained in favor with God, beloved and honored by all the angels. He could have used his noble powers to bless others and glorify Christ. But, as the prophet says, "Thine heart was lifted up because of thy beauty, thou hast corrupted thy wisdom by reason of thy brightness" (v. 17).

Little by little, Lucifer came to indulge a desire for self-exaltation. "Thou hast set thine heart as the heart of God." "Thou hast said, . . . I will exalt my throne above the stars of God: I will sit also upon the mount of the congregation. .... I will ascend above the heights of the clouds; I will be like the Most High" (v. 6; Isaiah 14:13, 14).

Instead of seeking to make God supreme in the affections and allegiance of His angels, Lucifer began trying to win their service and homage for himself. Lucifer wanted the honor that God, in His infinite wisdom, had given to Jesus alone. And so, in trying to take the power that belonged to Christ alone, the prince of angels rebelled against the very God who had made him. Worse yet, he convinced a large number of God's angels to join him in this ungrateful, horrible act.

Near-death experiences like Betty Eadie's are actually quite common. Many people have said how they were able to see themselves lying on a bed and watching doctors trying to revive them. Others have told stories about long tunnels with a bright, beautiful light shining in the distance. Still others have said they've spoken with dead loved ones. But some say near-death experiences can be attributed to the lack of oxygen getting to the brain, causing massive hallucinations where anything is possible as the brain struggles to live.

Final Thought

Feelings aren't evil. God gave us feelings to enrich our human experience and to bond closer to Him and one another. Just like reason apart from feelings brings hollow loyalty, feelings apart from reason lead to terrible dangers. Indeed, it was feelings that transformed Lucifer, an angel of light, into the cruel devil called Satan.

That's why Betty Eadie's ideas of the universe are so dangerous. They sound great and inviting, but behind these pleasant feelings are lies that Satan hopes you will buy into, because the more he can get you to accept his version of events, the more he can get you to disagree with what God wants from you.

Prior to the devil's rebellion, heaven was at peace and every created creature lived in harmony. Can you honestly say that you would rather have it the devil's way? Doesn't it make sense to desire the way God wants it to be for your life?

10

The Way
of Pride

erhaps no historical figure is as reviled as Adolph Hitler. He plunged the world into one of the bloodiest wars of history and engineered the decimation of millions of Jews and other "undesirables."

Yet not so many choose to remember the good that Hitler did for his country early in his career. Despite the ultimate vileness of his legacy, it is worth remembering that in the beginning, Germans loved Hitler for a reason. So while good people are certainly not fans of Hitler and do not wish to glorify him in any way, a well-worn saying does deserve consideration: "Study history or you will repeat it." And studying the legacy of Hitler, both good and bad, will also help us understand the devil.

Under Hitler, Germany grew strong and modern, an economic powerhouse, with industries that brought goods to every corner of the globe. Hitler built superhighways, among the best in the world, that spanned the width and breadth of his country. He built magnificent stadiums that hosted world-class events and helped create the country's first national car. As the people's car, it was the pride of Germany, a symbol that the country had earned its place among the industrialized nations of the world.

Indeed, there was nothing Germany couldn't do, and there was nothing Hitler could do wrong—or so it seemed. He was the symbol of Germany's virtue, strength, and greatness—the pride and joy of his country. Hitler was out to change his world, to conquer it for his Third Reich, to craft it in his own image.

By the time his people realized they had been duped by a madman, it was too late. Many who might not have ever hated Jews allowed themselves to be seduced by that madness and joined one of the worst genocides in history.

Likewise, in the early eons of the universe, Lucifer was a leader. Yet displeased at not being the highest authority, he began to have growing and sinister ambitions. Hitler also had aspirations. It wasn't enough for him to rule his country. He wanted to rule the world, and so he set out to create his "great society"—a country that would feature the "master race" and eliminate or subjugate all of its rivals.

Lucifer too wanted to change his world. Finding fault with the government of God, he wanted to set up a new order in heaven.

Before Lucifer began sowing his seeds of discontent, heaven had been full of joy. The angels' highest aspiration was to reflect their Creator's glory and show forth his praise. And while God was thus honored, all had been peace and gladness.

A note of discord now marred the celestial harmonies, however. The entrance of selfishness, which was so contrary to God's plan, awakened forebodings of evil in minds to whom God's glory was supreme.

The heavenly councils pleaded with Lucifer. The Son of God presented before him the greatness, the goodness, and the justice of the Creator, and the sacred, unchanging nature of His law. God Himself had established the order of heaven, and in departing from it, Lucifer would dishonor his Maker and bring ruin upon himself. But the warning, given in infinite love and mercy, only aroused a spirit of resistance. Lucifer allowed jealousy of Christ to prevail, and he became the more determined.

It was Lucifer's own pride—pride in his glory—that nourished the desire for supremacy. Lucifer didn't appreciate the high honors God had given him. Instead, glorying in his own brightness and exaltation, he aspired to be equal with God.

Lucifer was beloved and reverenced by the heavenly host. Angels delighted to execute his commands, and he was clothed with wisdom and glory above them all. Yet the Son of God was the acknowledged Sovereign of heaven, one in power and authority with the Father. In all the councils of God, Christ was a participant, while Lucifer was not permitted thus to enter into the divine purposes. "Why," questioned this mighty angel, "should Christ have the supremacy? Why is He thus honored above Lucifer?"

Leaving his place in the immediate presence of God, Lucifer went forth to sow seeds of discontent among the angels. At first, he worked with mysterious secrecy. For a time he concealed his real purpose, leading others to believe that by trying to make things better, he was really helping God.

Lucifer took issue with the laws that governed heavenly beings, suggesting that such restraints were really unnecessary. Since their natures were holy, he urged that the angels should obey their own will.

Lucifer also sought to create sympathy for himself by representing God had unjustly exalted Christ. He claimed that in aspiring to greater power and honor he was not aiming at self-exaltation, but was seeking to secure liberty for all the inhabitants of heaven, that by this means they might attain to a higher state of existence.

The mastermind behind the Holocaust, Hitler once said that people will believe a lie if you tell it big enough. He slowly built momentum by convincing Germans that Jews had taken control of the nation's economy and were unfairly wielding power over native Germans. He began by seizing assets and then later herded Jews into ghettos. He then led his people to believe that Jews were being evicted, all the while shipping them to concentration camps where they would be killed. Likewise, Lucifer uses often small, white lies to lead humans to believe the biggest lies of all.

The Patience of God

In His great mercy, God the Father bore long with Lucifer. The rebel angel was not immediately degraded from his exalted position. Lucifer retained his high position in heaven long after he began to indulge the spirit of discontent and present his false claims before the loyal angels.

Again and again Lucifer was offered pardon on condition of repentance and submission. Such efforts as only infinite love and wisdom could devise were made to convince him of his error. The spirit of discontent had never before been known in heaven. Lucifer himself did not at first see whither he was drifting; he did not understand the real nature of his feelings. But as his dissatisfaction was proved to be without cause, Lucifer was convinced that he was in the wrong, that the divine claims were just, and that he ought to acknowledge them as such before all heaven.

Had he done this, Lucifer might have saved himself and many angels. He had not at this time fully cast off his allegiance to God. Though he had forsaken his position as covering cherub, yet if he had been willing to return to God, acknowledge the Creator's wisdom, and fill the place appointed him in God's great plan, he would have been reinstated in his office. But pride forbade him to submit. He persistently defended his own course, maintained that he had no need of repentance, and fully committed himself, in the great controversy, against his Maker.

All the powers of Lucifer's mastermind were now bent to the work of deception, to secure the sympathy of the angels that had been under his command. Even the fact that Christ had warned and counseled him was perverted to serve his traitorous designs.

To those whose loving trust bound them most closely to him, Satan had represented that he was wrongly judged, that his position was not respected, and that his liberty was to be abridged. From misrepresentation of the words of Christ he passed to prevarication and direct falsehood, accusing the Son of God of a design to humiliate him before the inhabitants of heaven. He sought also to make a false issue between himself and the loyal angels.

Final Thought

For most people, it always boils down to pride—a dangerous focus on self. Hitler was a madman who drowned in his own pride, just like Satan. Here we see the evil depths to which pride will take a person, but the perils of pride aren't always so obvious to the infected.

People often hang on so strongly to their opinions for the sake of their honor. They don't want others to see them as ignorant or just plain wrong, so they fight truth and—perhaps like the German people—often convince themselves that lies are the truth.

Like the Germans, however, this kind of thinking mostly leads to unhappiness and discouragement. We might lie to those around us, but ultimately, we can't really lie to ourselves. That's why when we let go of pride, and cling to God's truth, relief washes over us. So be done with pride, accepting God's Word as the truth, letting go of traditional beliefs that will only harm you if you continue to treasure them in selfish pride.

11

The Biggest Liar of All

The Nazi regime had a ceaseless and highly effective propaganda machine. Dr. Joseph Goebbels, mastermind behind the barrage of images played to the German people, understood that people didn't want to just hear the news—they wanted to be entertained.

Thus the cinema was one of Goebbels' grandest assets. Color images were employed to enhance the military might of the Nazis, and thousands of Germans gathered at the events to see Hitler's addresses—the great orator in the hub of the incredible scenes.

Amid a sea of red flags, colossal marches and rallies were all placed in the very best light as evidence of the splendor of the Third Reich so that morale and patriotism were greatly increased. Movies like *Jud Suss,* the story of a Jew who instigated rape and torture, entertained audiences while reinforcing fears of popular stereotypes.

The tools of the propaganda machine were diverse and total. Through radio, television, newspapers, and the "Hitler Youth," the nazis infiltrated every aspect of peoples' lives. The Propaganda Ministry set guidelines for newspapers and punished journalists who broke the rules. The result was a highly successful image for Hitler, known as the "Hitler Myth," and credibility for the Nazi regime.

Unfortunately for the German people, much of the information and worldview they were being fed was wrong. The Nazi regime was not as powerful as it seemed on the silver screen, Hitler was not a caring man, and the Jewish people—rather than being instigators of torture and rape—were the victims.

Of course, the nazis certainly are not alone in twisting and misrepresenting facts to deceive others. Sad as it is, the first propaganda machine actually whirred into action thousands of years ago.

Lucifer, God's rebellious administrative assistant, was an expert at misleading others. He took revenge on the good angels who wouldn't take his side by accusing them of not caring about the interests of heavenly beings. The diabolical work that he himself was doing, he blamed on those who remained loyal to God.

One of Lucifer's biggest complaints was that God had been very unfair to him personally. Since there was really no truth to this allegation, Lucifer resorted to lies. He became an expert at misrepresenting the words and acts of the Creator. He loved to perplex the other angels with subtle arguments concerning the purposes of God.

Things that were really quite simple, Lucifer shrouded in mystery. By artfully perverting God's words, Lucifer succeeded in casting doubt on the plainest statements of Jehovah. Lucifer's high administrative position gave even greater weight to his lies. His dishonesty, wrong as it was, worked to his advantage. By misrepresenting the plain statements of God, Lucifer influenced many angels to join him in rebelling against heaven's authority.

In His great wisdom, God allowed Lucifer to carry forward his work until the spirit of discontent ripened into active rebellion. It was necessary for Lucifer's plans to be fully developed, that their true nature and tendency might be seen by all.

As the anointed cherub, Lucifer had been highly exalted. He was greatly loved by the heavenly angels, and his influence over them was strong. He had artfully presented his side of the question, relying on sophistry and fraud to persuade other angels. His power to deceive was very great, and by disguising himself in a cloak of falsehood he had gained an advantage. Even the loyal angels could not fully discern Lucifer's character or see where his work was leading.

Because Lucifer had been so highly honored, but now clothed all his acts in great mystery, it was difficult to disclose to the angels the true nature of his work. Until fully developed, sin didn't appear that evil.

Since sin had never had a place in God's universe before,

the angels had no conception of how truly degraded it was. They could not discern the terrible consequences that would result from setting aside divine law.

Lucifer had, at first, concealed his work under a specious profession of loyalty to God. He claimed to be seeking to promote the honor of God, the stability of His government, and the good of all the inhabitants of heaven. While instilling discontent into the minds of the angels under him, he had artfully made it appear that he was seeking to remove dissatisfaction.

Below-tje-Belt Tactics

Because of the nature of His character, God relied only on righteousness and truth in dealing with sin. Satan could use what God could not—flattery and deceit. He had tried to twist the Word of God, to misrepresent God's government before the angels. Lucifer claimed that, by making rules for the heavenly beings, God had been very unfair. He tried to convince anyone who would listen that God, in requiring obedience and submission from His creatures, was only exalting Himself.

In order to overturn the allegations of Lucifer, God needed to demonstrate before all heaven, as well as other worlds, that His government was fair, just, and true. Lucifer had artfully made it appear that he himself was promoting the good of the universe. The true character of the imposter, and his real goals, needed to be understood by all. And the only way this could happen was to allow time for Satan to demonstrate the wickedness of the principles he was promoting.

Even after it was decided that Lucifer must leave heaven, God didn't destroy him. Since only the service springing from love is acceptable to God, the allegiance of His subjects must rest on a conviction of God's justice and love.

At that time in the history of the universe, the inhabitants of heaven and other worlds didn't yet comprehend the nature or consequences of sin. They couldn't have seen the justice and mercy of God in the destruction of Satan.

If God had immediately blotted Satan from existence, the other created beings would have served Him from fear rather than from love. The influence of the deceiver would have remained, and the spirit of rebellion would have gone on.

Evil must be permitted to come to maturity. For the good of the entire universe in ages to come, Satan must develop his principles more fully. Then his accusations against the divine government can be seen in their true light by all created beings. Then and only then would the justice and mercy of God—and the unchangeable nature of His law—be forever placed beyond question.

Final Thought

Satan's propaganda machine is still running full throttle. If it weren't, we wouldn't be confused about God, and I wouldn't have had to struggle about what happened to my niece. But the fact is, lies are coming at us all the time.

Based on feelings, we'll often listen to the loudest person in the room. They command our attention and trust because they seem to have the guts to stand by what they believe. They put themselves on the line, we reason, so why would they be lying? But look at what happened to the angels who followed the devil . . . they listened to the noisy squeaky wheel, and now we're told it's too late for them.

But it's not too late for us. God isn't always the loudest person in the room, although He certainly can be. Instead, He offers us His Word in quiet study, always trying to speak to our reason. Let's get through the propaganda by studying God's Word together.

12

Why God Allowed Sin

On August 6, 1945, at 8:16 A.M., the atomic bomb "Fat Man" exploded above Hiroshima, Japan. Dropped from the Enola Gay, with the equivalent power of 20,000 tons of TNT, everything within four square miles was utterly destroyed.

The decision to drop the first atomic bomb has been debated ever since. Supporters argue that the bomb shortened the war and saved thousands of American lives. Indeed, casualty projections for invading the Japanese mainland ran into the hundreds of thousands. Opponents, on the other hand, say it was an unnecessary use of destructive power that killed civilians.

Yet other factors also contributed to the use of "Fat Man," and later "Little Boy" in Nagasaki, including an American public growing weary of the war and eager to see it end quickly. Moreover, Truman wanted to give Russia, on the hunt for war trophies, something to think about. Still, the most significant factor might simply have been that Truman didn't really have another good option in his "arsenal."

As the Japanese government was deeply divided on the subject of continued resistance, Truman's pro-war cabinet members insisted that Japan could mount a successful defense of its mainland. There was no guarantee that the Japanese would stop fighting, and thus the coming bloodshed was unavoidable. So he chose the bomb.

Obviously, the debate about the Hiroshima attack will go on forever. But with or without the bomb, some kind of carnage and suffering was unavoidable.

God and His subjects in heaven also came under attack—by Lucifer and his minions. The Creator didn't want a fight, but at the same time, He had to defend His kingdom from a cruel and deceptive power.

The options that Truman had to end the war would all end in bloodshed; likewise, when rebellion fomented in heaven, every choice at God's disposal seemed to lead to some kind of tragedy.

The Only Option

God could have snuffed Satan and his followers out right from the start. Doing so, however, would have defeated one of the basic principles of His universe—namely, that His creatures should serve Him willingly, out of love and respect for His character.

God's other option was to let Satan continue to exist for at least some period of time. During that trial period, Satan would be allowed to develop the principles he was promoting, and the entire universe would see where sin really led. The problem was that this option also involved bloodshed. There would be murders and wars, catastrophes and death, all as a natural result of sin.

Some people accuse God of being responsible for all the hurt in the world today, because He has the power to stop it yet hasn't done so. But in the long-range view of things, stopping sin before Satan has fully demonstrated what a failure it is would leave open the possibility that it might rise again.

Satan's rebellion was to be a lesson to the universe through all coming ages, a perpetual testimony to the nature and terrible results of sin. The working out of Satan's rule, its effects upon both men and angels, would demonstrate the results of setting aside divine authority. It would testify that the well-being of God's creatures is forever linked with His government and law.

Thus the history of this terrible experiment of rebellion was to be a perpetual safeguard to all holy intelligences, to prevent them from being deceived about the nature of transgression and to save them from committing sin and suffering its punishments.

Right up until the moment he was thrown from heaven's gates, Lucifer continued to justify his words and actions. When God announced that Lucifer and all his followers would be banished from heaven's bliss, the rebel leader also had an announcement to make. Publicly declaring his contempt for God's law, he reiterated his belief that angels need no control, but should be left to follow their own "inner self," which would ever guide into right actions.

Lucifer denounced the law of God as a restriction of angel liberty and confirmed his purpose to do away with God's law altogether. Then freed from this restraint, the hosts of heaven would enter into a more exalted, glorious state of existence.

Lucifer and his entire retinue of angels blamed their rebellion entirely on Christ, claiming that if they had not been reproved, they would never have rebelled. Still stubborn and defiant in their disloyalty, they tried in vain to overthrow the government of God. While still blasphemously claiming to be the innocent victims of oppressive power, the archrebel and all his sympathizers were at last banished from heaven.

Where Was the Battle Taken?

The same spirit that prompted rebellion in heaven still inspires rebellion on earth. Satan has continued with men the same policy that he pursued with the angels. His spirit now reigns in the children of disobedience. Like their leader, men seek to break down the restraints of God's law. Like their leader, men promise others liberty through transgression of the law. And just as it did in heaven, reproof of sin arouses the spirit of hatred and resistance.

When God pricks the conscience of men with messages of warning, Satan leads them to justify themselves and seek sympathy from others. Instead of correcting their errors, they become indignant against the reprover, as if he were the sole cause of difficulty. From the days of righteous Abel to our own time, the same spirit has been displayed against those who dare to call sin by its right name.

Satan is using the same tactics on earth that he used so successfully in heaven. By misrepresenting the character of God, Satan persuades men to regard their Creator as severe and tyrannical. Then, having succeeded in that, he declares that it is God's unjust restrictions that led to the fall of both humans and himself.

But the Eternal One Himself proclaims His character: "The Lord God, merciful and gracious, longsuffering, and abundant in goodness and truth, keeping mercy for thousands, forgiving iniquity and transgression and sin, and that will by no means clear the guilty" (Exodus 34:6, 7).

When God banished Satan from heaven, He declared His justice and maintained the honor of His throne. But when man sinned by yielding to the temptations of Satan, God showed what love really was by giving up His only Son to save the fallen race. In the cross of Christ, God's true character was revealed. The cross demonstrated to the universe once and for all that Lucifer, not God, was responsible for sin.

How God Won the Battle

During the earthly ministry of Christ, the character of the great deceiver was unmasked. Through his cruel warfare against the world's Redeemer, Satan effectually uprooted himself from the affections of the heavenly angels and the whole watching universe once and for all.

The daring blasphemy of his demand that Christ should bow down to him, his unholy boldness in carrying Christ to the mountain summit and the pinnacle of the temple, the diabolical intent shown by Satan in urging Christ to cast himself down from that dizzying height, the unsleeping malice that hunted Christ from place to place and finally inspired the hearts of priests and people to reject His love cry, "Crucify Him! Crucify Him!"—all this excited the amazement and indignation of the universe.

Satan was behind the world's rejection of Christ. When Satan saw the mercy and love of Jesus, His compassion and pitying tenderness, and how these were representing to the world the character of God—the prince of evil exerted all his power and cunning to destroy Jesus.

Satan made the life of Jesus hard. He contested every claim put forth by the Son of God and employed men to fill Christ's life with suffering and sorrow. The sophistry and falsehood by which he had sought to hinder the work of Jesus, the hatred manifested through the children of disobedience, the cruel accusations against Him whose life was one of unparalleled goodness, all sprang from deep-seated revenge.

The pent-up fires of envy and malice, hatred and revenge, burst forth on Calvary against the Son of God, while all heaven gazed upon the scene in silent horror.

When the great sacrifice was complete, Christ ascended to heaven, refusing the adoration of angels until He had presented the request: "I will that they also, whom Thou hast given Me, be with Me where I am" (John 17:24). Then with inexpressible love and power came forth the answer from the Father's throne: "Let all the angels of God worship Him" (Hebrews 1:6). Despite the utmost efforts of Satan, not one stain of sin rested upon Jesus. His humiliation was ended, His sacrifice complete, and in heaven there was given unto Him a name that is above every name.

Final Thought

Sometimes love hurts. My own kids have suffered for their mistakes, and as odd as it might seem at first—I'd rather they suffer and learn from their mistakes. I'm glad that I suffered for my mistakes, so that I might never go back to repeat them.

This isn't a perfect metaphor for why God allows sin, but it's a pretty good one. True love doesn't force itself and it never lies—read 1 Corinthians 13, and remember that God is love while you read it.

God knows that only true love like this will last eternally. If He forced His way on us, even if He was perfectly right, no one could honestly follow Him out of love—only out of fear. That's why He wants to us to choose right, just like He wanted Lucifer to choose right. He wants our love and respect, not our fear.

When we are misrepresented, we want everyone to know the truth about us. Yet when those people don't trust us, sometimes we need to let their error run its course. God is love, but Satan and humans didn't trust that part of Him. He is allowing Satan's error to play out, so that we can see why, in the end, his deceit will not win. He is letting evil takes its full course.

13

The Unmasking
of Satan

Ferdinand Waldo Demera Jr., made famous by the movie *The Great Imposter,* had to have been one of the world's greatest frauds. During the 1950s, Demera successfully worked as a professor, surgeon, monk, schoolteacher, and a prison warden—all with the FBI chasing his trail.

What made Demera's varied career truly amazing was that he was neither trained nor qualified in any of these professions. Demera's fraud was uncovered after he received publicity for an emergency on-deck surgery performed during the Korean War. When the story appeared in Canadian newspapers, Dr. Joseph Cyr, the doctor whose credentials Demera had "borrowed," started asking questions.

Demera was then discharged from the Canadian navy. Strangely, there is no record of any other punishment being meted out, and Demera concluded his colorful career as a minister of the gospel. Ironically, he was never accused of being an imposter in this role.

While it might seem unfair to compare a mere mortal like Demera to the devil, the two do have something in common. Demera may well have been "The Great Imposter," but Lucifer is the greatest imposter the universe has ever known.

Lucifer was so adept at twisting things to make it look like God was to blame, that, even after the fall of man, many heavenly angels were still unclear on the issues involved. It wasn't until the cross that Satan revealed his true character. There, his guilt stood out as never before. The angels of God and the watching worlds saw him for what he really was—a liar and murderer.

Angels and beings from other worlds saw the hateful spirit with which Satan ruled men, who were under his power, and knew that if heaven had come under his control, the same fate would have been theirs. Satan had claimed that breaking God's law would bring liberty and exaltation, but instead, it became clear that sin brought only bondage and degradation.

Satan's lying charges against the divine character and government appeared in their true light. When God had required the obedience and submission of His children, Satan accused the Creator of self-exaltation. Satan had freely declared that, while God exacted self-denial from others, He Himself practiced no self-denial, made no sacrifice.

This lie was upended at Calvary. At the foot of the cross, it became abundantly clear that the Ruler of the universe had made the greatest sacrifice that love could make, for "God was in Christ, reconciling the world unto Himself" (2 Corinthians 5:19). It was also seen that, while Lucifer had opened the door for the entrance of sin by his pride and hunger for power, Jesus had, in order to destroy sin, humbled Himself and became obedient unto death.

The principles of rebellion promoted by Satan were and still are repulsive to God, a fact that He demonstrated to the universe by making such an incredible sacrifice to banish those principles once and for all. For their part, all heaven understood the justice of God, both in the condemnation of Satan and the salvation of man.

Lucifer had declared that if the law of God was changeless, and its penalty could not be remitted, everyone who broke the law must be forever banned from God's favor. He had claimed that the sinful race was placed beyond redemption and therefore his rightful prey.

But the death of Christ was an argument in man's behalf that could not be overthrown. The penalty of the law fell on Him who was equal with God, making man free to accept the righteousness of Christ and triumph, just as Jesus had triumphed, over the power of Satan. This is how God can be both just, and yet the justifier of all who believe in Jesus.

What Happens When the War Ends?

When judgment is finally executed on the devil and his angels, it will be seen once and for all that there is no good reason for sin.

When the Judge of all the earth shall demand of Satan, "Why have you rebelled against Me, and robbed Me of the subjects of My kingdom?" the originator of evil will be without excuse. Every mouth will be stopped, and all the hosts of rebellion will be speechless.

The cross of Calvary, while showing that God's law is unchangeable, also proclaims to the universe that the wages of sin is death. In the Savior's expiring cry, "It is finished," the death knell of Satan was rung (John 19:30).

The great controversy that had been so long in progress was then decided, and the final eradication of evil was made certain. The Son of God passed through the portals of the tomb, that "through death He might destroy him that had the power of death, that is, the devil" (Hebrews 2:14).

Lucifer's desire for self-exaltation had led him to say, "I will exalt my throne above the stars of God. . . . I will be like the Most High" (Isaiah 14:13, 14). God declares, "I will bring thee to ashes upon the earth . . . and never shalt thou be any more" (Ezekiel 28:18, 19).

When "the day cometh, that shall burn as an oven; . . . all the proud, yea, and all that do wickedly, shall be stubble: and the day that cometh shall burn them up, saith the Lord of hosts, that it shall leave them neither root nor branch" (Malachi 4:1).

The whole universe will have become witnesses to the nature and results of sin. And its utter extermination, which in the beginning would have brought fear to angels and dishonor to God, will now vindicate His love and establish His honor before the universe of beings who delight to do His will, and in whose heart is His law.

Sin will be gone forever, never to come back again. "Affliction shall not rise up the second time" (Nahum 1:9).

The law of God, which Satan has sneered at as a yoke of bondage, will be honored as the law of liberty. A tested and proved creation will never again be turned from allegiance to Him whose character has been fully shown before them to be fathomless love and infinite wisdom.[11]

The Bible says that God is not the author of confusion, so why are we so confused about what happens when we die? If He's not the author of confusion, how come so many people don't know what happened to Katie when she died? Even the Christian church itself is in confusion. Betty Eadie believes that everyone's soul has always been around, while others in the church believe much differently.

Wouldn't it be better for everyone to know exactly what happens? I think so. Knowing the truth is perhaps the highest ideal, because it allows us to make the most of our lives.

It's important to know what you just read because now we understand why there is so much confusion, and why it is important to dig for the truth. We know that God would rather we hear and accept the truth, and why the devil is so interested in us being tricked.

Apparently, the deceits Satan used in heaven are the same ones he's using to trick us into believing his version of events. In the war in heaven, Satan convinced intelligent angels who lived among God that the Creator was a liar. How well might Satan do to convince us that what the Bible says can't be trusted?

The death of a loved one is a severe emotional drain. It is here that we are most vulnerable and most incapable of being reasonable. How can we be reasonable when our world just fell apart around us? How can we be sane when evil is taking the lives of little girls like Katie and leaving parents with empty hearts?

This is exactly why knowing the truth is so important. Otherwise, at our most vulnerable, Satan can make us believe and do anything as long as what he says sounds comforting and sincere in our time of need.

But God wants us to know the simple truth, and He's offered just that in the Bible. It's clear that within the pages of that book, we can build a solid foundation explaining what happens when we die.

Final Thought

God is not the author of confusion. Although knowing Him requires effort, He makes Himself perfectly clear to those who honestly seek Him. If we really want all the truth and none of the lies, we must study the Bible prayerfully, understanding that His total message on any given subject is from many parts of the Bible.

The same is true about death. The devil takes one Scripture about death and bends it so that it sounds like the whole truth. This can be avoided if we take everything the Bible says about death and the soul and let them fall into place.

By doing this, we unmask Satan's lies, and we find ourselves not only knowing the truth, but having fuller lives awash in peace and joy.

14

Are Our Loved Ones
Among Us?

On March 31, 1848, Kate and Margaretta Fox, ages 11 and 13, started down a path that would one day lead them to be considered the founders of the modern spiritualist movement. The Fox sisters are best known for "spirit rapping," a technique that uses a sequential knocking "code" to transmit messages to the other side of the spiritual veil.

The Fox sisters wowed local residents by demonstrating the phenomenon, and claimed to be communicating with Charles Haynes, a previous tenant of their home who said he had been murdered and buried under the house. The story reached its climax when bones turned up where the spirit claimed they laid. The two sisters became overnight sensations, and the spiritualism movement spread like wildfire around the world, thanks in part to P. T. Barnum.

The Fox Sisters eventually endured plenty of criticism, fell on hard times, and by 1888 had renounced their claims of special powers. At one point they claimed they'd fooled everyone by simply cracking their toes to mimic rapping sounds from the dead. A year later the sisters retracted that confession.

Skeptics claim the sisters died destitute alcoholics and were nothing more than frauds cashing in on gullible people. Believers still maintain the truth of the sisters' original story, and spiritualism today has hundreds of thousands of followers that can be traced back to the Fox sisters.

Whether or not the Fox sisters retracted their story is really beside the point. People can retract stories for many reasons—money, embarrassment, and fame, among others. The point is to determine if what they claimed to happen really can happen. Can the dead speak with us? Do they have the power to transcend heaven, like the angels, and affect our lives directly? Do we go on living after we die?

Another question I had is if the dead really can speak to us, why don't they speak to us personally? Must they always go through some spirit specialist, especially when it concerns very private and personal matters? Is it fair for God to allow my dead loved one to appear to and communicate with someone else, when they could just as easily speak to me?

After Katie died, the local community had a memorial service where they planted a tree in her honor. A lady who claimed to have been in communication with Katie came to that service, and found her way to Gary, Katie's grieving father.

At some point in the conversation, this mysterious lady pointed to where Wendell and Linda (Gary's in-laws) were standing, and asked, "Gary, who is that lady standing with that man (his father-in-law) in the denim shirt." Gary answered, "That's his wife, Linda."

"No," said the lady. "The other person—the gray-haired lady who is bent over."

Gary peered across the room but didn't see anybody fitting that description. However, the lady had given him a description that reminded him a lot of Wendell's mother, Grandma Scott. The spirit medium went on to tell Gary that she had seen what happened right after Katie's accident. According to her, the same lady she saw standing next to Wendell was at the accident, reaching out her hand to Katie. Katie reached up, grabbed the elderly lady's hand, and went with her to heaven.

That sounds wonderfully promising, for sure. But it highlights the point: Why and how did that medium get to see what I would have liked to see—something that doesn't even pertain to her?

But the ultimate question is even more important. How can we really know if she is telling the truth? Or since the medium really didn't know Katie or Grandma Scott, how could Gary know who the lady was really seeing? In this case, Gary and Heidi didn't know this woman before Katie's death. Was she a benign person with a message truly from God, or was she crafting some kind of deceit?

We've come to the point were we find out, from the Bible, exactly what happens to those we love when they die and how they interact with us. This is the place where my journey to discover what happened to my precious niece would come full circle. My questions would be answered, and the matter would be solved. No more confusion or worry. The journey up to this point has been well worth it, because we've built a foundation we can stand on—the Bible— but we've come to the point where an answer is now necessary and unavoidable.

What happened to Katie when she died? Is she with the angels in heaven? Is she watching down over her loved ones? We will need to journey a little more together and discover some amazing truths, but the answers to these questions will become clear to you as you read.

15

Deceived About Death?

With the earliest history of man, Satan began his efforts to deceive our race. He who had incited rebellion in heaven desired to bring the inhabitants of the earth to unite with him in his warfare against the government of God.

Adam and Eve had been perfectly happy in obedience to the law of God, and this fact was a constant testimony against the claim, which Satan had urged in heaven, that God's law was oppressive and opposed to the good of His creatures. And furthermore, Satan's envy was excited as he looked upon the beautiful home prepared for the sinless pair. He determined to cause their fall, that, having separated them from God and brought them under his own power, he might gain possession of the earth and here establish his kingdom in opposition to the Most High.

Had Satan revealed himself in his real character, he would have been repulsed at once, for Adam and Eve had been warned against this dangerous foe; but he worked in the dark, concealing his purpose, that he might more effectually accomplish his object.

Employing as his medium the serpent, then a creature of fascinating appearance, he addressed himself to Eve: "Hath God said, Ye shall not eat of every tree of the garden?" (Genesis 3:1). Had Eve refrained from entering into argument with the tempter, she would have been safe; but she ventured to parley with him and fell a victim to his wiles. It is thus that many are still overcome. They doubt and argue concerning the requirements of God; and instead of obeying the divine commands, they accept human theories, which but disguise the devices of Satan.

What Was the Devil's First Lie to Humans?

"The woman said unto the serpent, We may eat of the fruit of the trees of the garden: but of the fruit of the tree which is in the midst of the garden, God hath said, Ye shall not eat of it, neither shall ye touch it, lest ye die. And the serpent said unto the woman, Ye shall not surely die: for God doth know that in the day ye eat thereof, then your eyes shall be opened, and ye shall be as gods, knowing good and evil" (Genesis 3:2-5).

Satan declared that they would become like God, possessing greater wisdom than before and being capable of a higher state of existence. Eve yielded to temptation; and through her influence, Adam was led into sin. They accepted the words of the serpent, that God did not mean what He said; they distrusted their Creator and imagined that He was restricting their liberty and that they might obtain great wisdom and exaltation by transgressing His law.

But what did Adam, after his sin, find to be the meaning of the words, "In the day that thou eatest thereof thou shalt surely die?" Did he find them to mean, as Satan had led him to believe, that he was to be ushered into a more exalted state of existence? Then indeed there was great good to be gained by transgression, and Satan was proved to be a benefactor of the race.

But Adam did not find this to be the meaning of the divine sentence. God declared that as a penalty for his sin, man should return to the ground whence he was taken: "Dust thou art, and unto dust shalt thou return" (v. 19). The words of Satan, "Your eyes shall be opened," proved to be true in this sense only: After Adam and Eve had disobeyed God, their eyes were opened to discern their folly; they did know evil, and they tasted the bitter fruit of transgression.

What Is the Tree of Life?

In the midst of Eden grew the tree of life, whose fruit had the power of perpetuating life. Had Adam remained obedient to God, he would have continued to enjoy free access to this tree and would have lived forever. But when he sinned he was cut off from partaking of the tree of life, and he became subject to death. The divine sentence, "Dust thou art, and unto dust shalt thou return," points to the utter extinction of life.

Immortality, promised to man on condition of obedience, had

been forfeited by transgression. Adam could not transmit to his posterity that which he did not possess; and there could have been no hope for the fallen race had not God, by the sacrifice of His Son, brought immortality within their reach.

While "death passed upon all men, for that all have sinned," Christ "hath brought life and immortality to light through the gospel" (Romans 5:12; 2 Timothy 1:10). And only through Christ can immortality be obtained. Said Jesus, "He that believeth on the Son hath everlasting life: and he that believeth not the Son shall not see life" (John 3:36). Every man may come into possession of this priceless blessing if he will comply with the conditions. All "who by patient continuance in well-doing seek for glory and honor and immortality" will receive "eternal life" (Romans 2:7).

The only one who promised Adam life in disobedience was the great deceiver. And the declaration of the serpent to Eve in Eden— "Ye shall not surely die"—was the first sermon ever preached upon the immortality of the soul. Yet this declaration, resting solely upon the authority of Satan, is echoed from the pulpits of Christendom and is received by the majority of mankind as readily as it was received by our first parents. The divine sentence, "The soul that sinneth, it shall die" (Ezekiel 18:20) is made to mean: The soul that sinneth, it shall not die, but live eternally. We cannot but wonder at the strange infatuation that renders men so credulous concerning the words of Satan and so unbelieving in regard to the words of God.

Soon after their startling paranormal claims, Margaretta and Kate Fox were making a fortune at public appearances and private medium consultations, enjoying incredible celebrity status. But barely five years later, they had fallen into alcoholism, lost most of their money, and created controversy by admitting to faking the event that made them famous. Shortly, after their fall from grace, the two sisters were buried in a pauper's grave when they died.

Had man after his fall been allowed free access to the tree of life, he would have lived forever, and thus sin would have been immortalized. But cherubim and a flaming sword kept "the way of the tree of life" (Genesis 3:24), and not one of the family of Adam has been permitted to pass that barrier and partake of the life-giving fruit. Therefore, there is not an immortal sinner.

Final Thought

We are constantly being told to seek the truth about ourselves, to understand who we are a little better and where we came from so that we understand where we are going.

This chapter has revealed a great deal about who we really are, and thereby unmasked one of Satan's most dangerous lies. However, I encourage you never just to settle for an answer. No matter how good it feels, do your homework. Just like you would in buying a car or a house, you're going to do some research before you make a purchase.

How much more important is it to do this for your own soul? Check everything you hear and see by what the Bible says. Find out the facts, and then make your choice. If you want the truth, this is the only way you can do it.

And remember, misery loves company. A miserable devil is doing all he can to make you feel good that you will deceive yourself and end up being miserable. Don't fall for that!

16

The Truth
About Hell

The vast majority of churchgoers have never heard a sermon like the one for which Jonathan Edwards is most famous. Edwards was a renowned Puritan preacher, philosopher, theologian, and intellectual figure of colonial America. He graduated from Yale at age 17, became a preacher like his father and grandfather, and is today considered a theological titan of a caliber equaling Augustine, Luther, and Calvin.

Edward's famous six-hour sermon, "Sinners in the Hands of an Angry God," was delivered during "The Great Awakening." At that time in U.S. history, revival was sweeping the continent and thousands were daily coming to Christ. Some 250 years later, Edward's sermon is generally recognized as one of the greatest sermons ever preached on the North American continent.

Amazingly, Edwards was not a charismatic orator—he merely read his sermons. Yet he also believed that in order for lost sinners to come to Christ, they must first understand the desperate state they are in and the horrendous eternal consequences that accompany it. Edwards brought many of his listeners to this realization that day with "remarkable effect." Such was the power and passion of his words that moans and groans filled the sanctuary and people fainted as he spoke.

Using the words hell, fire, and brimstone generously throughout his sermon, Edwards provided convincing support for his awesomely graphic metaphors. As a result, his sermon elicited a sense of urgency rarely heard in church pulpits today.

In his famous sermon Jonathan Edwards somehow managed to drive home to his listeners that hell is an eternally fearful place, a place to be dreaded and avoided at all costs. His verbal pictures of torment, vengeance, and judgment were enough to bring an entire congregation to tears and a sense of anguish over their doomed condition.

While God uses ministers such as Edwards to awaken Christians from their sleeping, Satan is an expert at twisting the truth to make God look bad. The devil is especially adept at deceiving people on the topics of death, eternal torment, and immortality.

The Devil's Pictures

Right after Adam and Eve sinned, Satan instructed his angels to make a special effort to convince man of his natural immortality. Once the devil had succeeded in convincing men of this error, he and his angels went on to convince people that sinners would live in eternal misery.

Now the prince of darkness, working through his agents, represents God as a revengeful tyrant, declaring that He plunges into hell all those who do not please Him, and causes them ever to feel His wrath; and that while they suffer unutterable anguish and writhe in the eternal flames, their Creator looks down upon them with satisfaction.

Thus the archfiend clothes with his own attributes the Creator and Benefactor of mankind. Cruelty is satanic. God is love; and all that He created was pure, holy, and lovely, until sin was brought in by the first great rebel.

Satan himself is the enemy who tempts man to sin, and then destroys him if he can; and when he has made sure of his victim, then he exults in the ruin he has wrought. If permitted, he would sweep the entire race into his net. Were it not for the intervention of divine power, not one son or daughter of Adam would escape.

Satan is seeking to overcome men today. He overcame our first parents by shaking their confidence in their Creator and leading them to doubt the wisdom of His government and the justice of His laws, and he wants to deceive you.

The Ultimate Spin Doctor

In order to justify their malicious nature and rebellion, Satan and his angels love to represent God as even worse than themselves. The devil tries to shift blame for his own horrible cruelty of character upon our heavenly Father, so it will look like Satan was greatly wronged when God expelled him from heaven for not submitting to the heavenly governor.

Satan wants the world to believe that they will enjoy much liberty under his mild rule, in contrast with the bondage imposed by the stern decrees of Jehovah. Thus he succeeds in luring souls away from their allegiance to God.

How repulsive to every emotion of love and mercy, and even to our sense of justice, is the doctrine that the wicked dead are tormented with fire and brimstone in an eternally burning hell; that for the sins of a brief earthly life they are to suffer torture as long as God shall live. Yet this doctrine has been widely taught and is still embodied in many of the creeds of Christendom.

Said a learned doctor of divinity: "The sight of hell's torments will exalt the happiness of the saints forever. When they see others who are of the same nature and born under the same circumstances, plunged in such misery, and they so distinguished, it will make them sensible of how happy they are."

Another used these words: "While the decree of reprobation is eternally executing on the vessels of wrath, the smoke of their torment will be eternally ascending in view of the vessels of mercy, who, instead of taking the part of these miserable objects, will say, Amen, Alleluia! Praise ye the Lord!"

Where, in the pages of God's Word, is such teaching to be found? Will the redeemed in heaven be lost to all emotions of pity and compassion, and even to feelings of common humanity? Are these to be exchanged for the indifference of the stoic or the cruelty of the savage? No, no; such is not the teaching of the Book of God.

Those who present the views expressed in the quotations given above may be learned and even honest men, but they are deluded by the sophistry of Satan. He leads them to misinterpret strong expressions of Scripture, giving to the language the coloring of bitterness and malignity that pertains to himself, but not to our Creator. "As I live, saith the Lord God, I have no pleasure in the death of the wicked; but that the wicked turn from his way and live: turn ye, turn ye from your evil ways; for why will ye die?" (Ezekiel 33:11).

Does God Want Hell?

What would God gain if we believed that He delights in witnessing unceasing tortures; that He is regaled with the groans and shrieks and imprecations of the suffering creatures whom He holds in the flames of hell?

Can these horrid sounds be music in the ear of Infinite Love? It is urged that the infliction of endless misery upon the wicked would show God's hatred of sin as an evil that is ruinous to the peace and order of the universe. Oh, dreadful blasphemy! As if God's hatred of sin is the reason why it is perpetuated. For according to the teachings of these theologians, continued torture without hope of mercy maddens its wretched victims, and as they pour out their rage in curses and blasphemy, they are forever augmenting their load of guilt. God's glory is not enhanced by sin that continues throughout the ceaseless ages.

It is beyond the power of the human mind to estimate the evil that has been wrought by the heresy of eternal torment. The religion of the Bible, full of love and goodness, and abounding in compassion, is darkened by superstition and clothed with terror. When we consider in what false colors Satan has painted the character of God, can we wonder that our merciful Creator is feared, dreaded, and even hated? The appalling views of God that have spread over the world from the teachings of the pulpit have made thousands, yes, millions, of skeptics and infidels.

The theory of eternal torment is one of the false doctrines that constitute the wine of the abomination of Babylon, of which she makes all nations drink (Revelation 14:8; 17:2). The idea that ministers of Christ should have accepted this heresy and proclaimed it from the pulpit is indeed a mystery. True, it has been taught by great and good men; but the light on this subject had not come to them as it has come to us. They were responsible only for the light that shone in their time; we are accountable for that which shines in our day.

If we turn from the testimony of God's Word, and accept false doctrines because our fathers taught them, we fall under the condemnation pronounced upon Babylon; we are drinking of the wine of her abomination.

Final Thought

We've just unmasked another lie from Satan, and as a result, we continue to lay the foundation of truth toward learning what happened to Katie.

But I don't want you to miss something. By unmasking Satan a little bit more, we've learned something rather amazing about God. And by doing this, we are closer to seeing Him for who He really is—a God of pure love who wants to be with His creation.

If you didn't get a rush of joy while reading this chapter, I urge you to read it again. Not only does it open up more secrets beyond the grave, the truth of it will give you amazing peace about your loved ones—whether they were believers or not.

17

The Unsinkable Theory

"God himself could not sink this ship," boasted a crew member aboard the 46,000-ton Titanic, an opulently appointed ocean liner larger than any ship ever built before. With its 16 watertight compartments, the remarkable ship reflected the day's most advanced engineering techniques.

Boasting such luxurious features as Turkish baths and wide verandas flanked with potted palms, fine dining, and the best orchestra afloat, the Titanic was virtually a world unto itself, insensible to the buffeting of wind and wave.

On April 10, 1912, the gigantic luxury craft sailed toward New York from Southampton, England, carrying more than 2,200 people. Some were enormously wealthy, others were immigrants in steerage class, but most were confident that their passage across the treacherous North Atlantic would be worry free.

Benjamin and Esther Hart, together with their daughter Eva, were aboard the Titanic on that fateful voyage. They had planned to travel aboard the Philadelphia, but their passage was cancelled by a coal strike. And so the family was transferred to the Titanic, much to the displeasure of Esther.

"Now I know why I feel so uneasy," she said as she arrived on deck. "This is the ship everyone is saying is unsinkable."

"No my dear," Benjamin said, putting his arm around her shoulders. "This is the ship *that is* unsinkable." Esther gave him a long, hard look.

"Well, that is flying in the face of God," she answered, and she refused to sleep that night.

On April 14, the Titanic received at least six warnings about icebergs. Still it continued at breakneck speed, making no allowance for the treacherous waters just over the horizon.

Less than 24 hours later, two collapsible rafts and 15 lifeboats were scattered among fields of icebergs in the choppy, frigid waters of the Atlantic. Amid the drifting debris, hundreds of battered and bruised corpses floated face up, most already rendered unrecognizable. To one observer, they looked like a flock of seagulls bobbing in the waves. Many were women, rigidly clutching their babies in death.

The lifeboats carried the roughly third of the passengers who were still alive. Half frozen, exhausted from shock, the survivors were fragile proof that the great Titanic had once existed—before sinking forever into the night. The world's first "unsinkable" ship had foundered and vanished within hours of its brush with a silent, unyielding iceberg.

Esther and Eva Hart survived the sinking, but Benjamin went down with the Titanic.

Many people today are as oblivious to the truth about hell and eternal torment as those individuals were, so many years ago, about the "mortality" of the Titanic. It's all too easy to believe what we want to believe, or to go along with popular opinion, even when evidence points in the opposite direction. Sometimes we find one idea so revolting that, in trying to form our true opinion, we are driven to the opposite error.

This is certainly the case with people who find the idea of eternal torment to be particularly appalling. In their efforts to avoid that error, they are tempted to jump off the deep end in the opposite direction.

The Unsinkable Human

They see that the Bible represents God as full of love and compassion, and they can't believe that He will consign His creatures to the fires of an eternally burning hell.

They still insist that the soul is naturally immortal, however. As a result, and in order to reconcile their beliefs, they see no alternative but to believe that all mankind will be saved in the end.

Many think the threatenings of the Bible were designed merely to frighten men into obedience, and not to be literally fulfilled. Thus the sinner can live in selfish pleasure, disregarding the requirements of God, and yet expect to be finally received into His favor. Such a doctrine, presuming upon God's mercy, but ignoring His justice, pleases the carnal heart and makes the wicked bolder in their sin.

Believers in universal salvation wrest the Scriptures to sustain their soul-destroying theories. For example, at the funeral of an irreligious young man who had been killed instantly by an accident, a minister chose as his text the Scripture statement concerning David: "He was comforted concerning Amnon, seeing he was dead" (2 Samuel 13:39).

"I am frequently asked," said the speaker, "what will be the fate of those who leave the world in sin, die, perhaps, in a state of inebriation, die with the scarlet stains of crime unwashed from their robes, or die as this young man died, having never made a profession or enjoyed an experience of religion. We are content with the Scriptures; their answer shall solve the awful problem. Amnon was exceedingly sinful; he was unrepentant, he was made drunk, and while drunk was killed. David was a prophet of God; he must have known whether it would be ill or well for Amnon in the world to come. What were the expressions of his heart? 'The soul of King David longed to go forth unto Absalom: for he was comforted concerning Amnon, seeing he was dead.' "

The minister deduced from this verse that David was comforted because he, as a prophet, could look forward into the glorious future and see his son far removed from all temptations, released from the bondage of sin. Then, after Amnon was made sufficiently holy and enlightened, he could be admitted to the assembly of ascended and rejoicing spirits.

According to this minister, David was comforted by knowing that Amnon had been removed from the present state of sin and suffering, and sent to a place where the loftiest breathings of the Holy Spirit would be shed upon his darkened soul, where his mind would be unfolded to the wisdom of heaven and the sweet raptures of immortal love, and thus prepared with a holy nature to enjoy the rest and society of the heavenly inheritance.

The Fruits of Error

If we believe the teachings of this minister, we must then conclude that the salvation of heaven depends upon nothing that we can do in this life; neither upon a present change of heart, nor upon present belief, or a present profession of religion.

Unfortunately, this professed minister of Christ was repeating the falsehood first uttered by the serpent in Eden, "Ye shall not surely die. In the day ye eat thereof, then your eyes shall be opened, and ye shall be as gods." He declares that the vilest of sinners—the murderer, the thief, and the adulterer—will after death be prepared to enter into immortal bliss.

And from what does this perverter of the Scriptures draw his conclusions? From a single sentence expressing David's submission to the dispensation of Providence. His soul "longed to go forth unto Absalom: for he was comforted concerning Amnon, seeing he was dead."

The poignancy of his grief having been softened by time, his thoughts turned from the dead to the living son, self-banished through fear of the just punishment of his crime. And this is the evidence that the incestuous, drunken Amnon was at death immediately transported to the abodes of bliss, there to be purified and prepared for the companionship of sinless angels! A pleasing fable indeed, well suited to gratify the carnal heart! This is Satan's own doctrine, and it does his work effectually. Should we be surprised that, with such instruction, wickedness abounds?

The course pursued by this one false teacher illustrates that of many others. A few words of Scripture are separated from the context, which would in many cases show their meaning to be exactly opposite to the interpretation put upon them; and such disjointed passages are perverted and used in proof of doctrines that have no foundation in the Word of God.

The testimony cited as evidence that the drunken Amnon is in heaven directly contradicts the plain and positive statement of the Scriptures that no drunkard shall inherit the kingdom of God (1 Corinthians 6:10). It is thus that doubters, unbelievers, and skeptics turn the truth into a lie. And multitudes have been deceived by their sophistry and rocked to sleep in the cradle of carnal security.

If it is true that the souls of all men pass directly to heaven at the hour of their demise, then we might well covet death rather than life. Many have been led by this belief to put an end to their existence. When overwhelmed with trouble, perplexity, and disappointment, it seems an easy thing to break the brittle thread of life and soar away into the bliss of the eternal world.

In His Word, God has given decisive evidence that He will punish the transgressors of His law. Those who flatter themselves that He is too merciful to execute justice upon the sinner have only to look to the cross of Calvary.

The death of the spotless Son of God testifies that "the wages of sin is death," that every violation of God's law must receive its just retribution. Christ the sinless became sin for man. He bore the guilt of transgression, and the hiding of His Father's face, until His heart was broken and His life crushed out.

All this sacrifice was made that sinners might be redeemed. In no other way could man be freed from the penalty of sin. And every soul who refuses to become a partaker of the atonement provided at such a cost must bear in his own person the guilt and punishment of transgression.

Final Thought

As with the Titanic, man likes to put his faith in things of his own building. But in our selfish pride, we have fooled ourselves into thinking that our ships of reason are somehow unsinkable.

This has caused us to believe things that have put our own safety at risk. Thankfully, we have a life raft that can get us through the choppy waters of lies and half-truths. We have the Bible, and I pray that you will learn to trust in God.

He is the only unsinkable thing we have in this world. Cling to Him and His safety, and you will live in eternity.

18

Where the Wicked
Dead Really Go

Perhaps nothing is more revealing about society's fixation with life after death than the 2005 television season line-up. According to the Sunday, June 19 edition of *The Detroit Free Press,* "you don't have to be a psychic to detect a supernatural vibe emanating from the fall TV season. Prime time will be doing the paranormal polka as six new network series with supernatural, horror, or sci-fi themes give the fall season its signature programming trend."

All in all, six new shows revolve around either extraterrestrial beings and/or the supernatural. According to *The Free Press,* "ABC's breakout, buzz-generating suspense drama about castaways on a very strange South Pacific island is a key inspiration for the new wave of supernatural-ized fall programming. And NBC's quirky surprise hit *Medium,* the stories of a psychic suburban mom who fights crime, may have joined *Lost* as an influence in the supernatural trend."

But don't you think that while the "fall full of fright nights" can certainly be entertaining to some folks, television as a whole is a poor place to go for answers to any of life's deepest questions? If show writers are trying to impart truth, and there are so many different versions of what happens in the spirit world, how can we know what is true from false from television?

As a student, you might have been fortunate enough to have a math book where answers to odd or even questions were provided in the back of the book. Maybe you have even been lucky enough to stumble across the "Teacher's Edition," where answers were provided throughout the entire textbook.

Christians need to treat the Bible as the "Teacher's Edition" for life. It provides answers to life's questions through its pages. I've learned that finding answers to questions about where the dead really go in Hollywood productions is about as likely as finding democracy in the heart of a communist country. It just isn't there. We can find answers, however, by turning to our Bibles. Let us consider a little further what the Bible teaches concerning people who are ungodly and unrepentant.

Answers From "The Book"

Many religions today teach that such people are in heaven, living as holy, happy angels. But is this true? God's Word does promise to give us the answers—if we search for them—for the Bible says, "I will give unto him that is athirst of the fountain of the water of life freely" (Revelation 21:6).

This promise is only to those who thirst. None but those who feel their need of the water of life, and seek it at the loss of all things else, will be supplied. "He that overcometh shall inherit all things; and I will be his God, and he shall be My son" (v.7).

Although the water of life is available to all, there are conditions that must be met. In order to inherit all things, we must resist and overcome sin.

The Lord declares by the prophet Isaiah: "Say ye to the righteous, that it shall be well with him. Woe unto the wicked! it shall be ill with him: for the reward of his hands shall be given him" (Isaiah 3:10, 11).

"Though a sinner do evil an hundred times," says the wise man, "and his days be prolonged, yet surely I know that it shall be well with them that fear God, which fear before Him: but it shall not be well with the wicked" (Ecclesiastes 8:12, 13).

And Paul testifies that the sinner is treasuring up unto himself "wrath against the day of wrath and revelation of the righteous judgment of God; who will render to every man according to his deeds; . . . tribulation and anguish upon every soul of man that doeth evil" (Romans 2:5, 6, 9).

What Does God's Word Say About Who Goes Where?

"No fornicator, nor unclean person, nor covetous man, who is an idolater, hath any inheritance in the kingdom of Christ and God"

(Ephesians 5:5). "Follow peace with all men, and holiness, without which no man shall see the Lord" (Hebrews 12:14).

"Blessed are they that do His commandments, that they may have right to the tree of life, and may enter in through the gates into the city. For without are dogs, and sorcerers, and whoremongers, and murderers, and idolaters, and whosoever loveth and maketh a lie" (Revelation 22:14, 15).

God has given men a declaration of His character and His method of dealing with sin. "The Lord God, merciful and gracious, longsuffering and abundant in goodness and truth, keeping mercy for thousands, forgiving iniquity and transgression and sin, and that will by no means clear the guilty" (Exodus 34:6, 7). "All the wicked will He destroy" (Psalms 145:20). "The transgressors shall be destroyed together: the end of the wicked shall be cut off" (Psalm 37:38).

Although God will utilize the power and authority of His divine government to put down rebellion, even the judgments of God will be perfectly consistent with His character as a merciful, longsuffering, and benevolent being.

God does not force the will or judgment of any. He takes no pleasure in slavish obedience. He wants the creatures of His hands to love Him because He is worthy of love. He wants them to obey Him because they have an intelligent appreciation of His wisdom, justice, and benevolence. And all who understand these qualities will love Him because they are drawn toward Him in admiration of His attributes.

The principles of kindness, mercy, and love, taught by Christ and exemplified by His life, are a transcript of the will and character of God. Jesus declared that He taught nothing except that which He had received from His Father. The principles of the divine government are in perfect harmony with the command of Jesus to "love your enemies."

God executes justice upon the wicked for the good of the universe and even for the good of those upon whom His judgments are visited. He would make them happy if He could do so in accordance with the laws of His government and the justice of His character. He surrounds them with the tokens of His love, He grants them a knowledge of His law, and follows them with the offers of His mercy; but they despise His love, make void His law, and reject His mercy.

While constantly receiving His gifts, they dishonor the Giver; they hate God because they know that He abhors their sins. The Lord bears long with their perversity; but the decisive hour will come at last, when their destiny is to be decided. Will He then chain these rebels to His side? Will He force them to do His will?

Why Doesn't Every Soul Go to Heaven?

Those who have chosen Satan as their leader and have been controlled by his power are not prepared to enter the presence of God. Pride, deception, licentiousness, and cruelty have become fixed in their characters.

How could wicked ones ever enter heaven and live there forever with those they despised and hated on earth? Truth will never be agreeable to a liar; the proud and self-confident will not suddenly become meek; purity is not acceptable to the corrupt; and selfless love doesn't appear attractive to the selfish. What source of enjoyment could heaven offer to those who are wholly absorbed in earthly and selfish interests?

Could those whose lives have been spent in rebellion against God be suddenly transported to heaven and witness the high, holy state of perfection that ever exists there—every soul filled with love, every countenance beaming with joy, enrapturing music in melodious strains rising in honor of God and the Lamb, and ceaseless streams of light flowing upon the redeemed from the face of Him who sits upon the throne—could those whose hearts are filled with hatred of God, of truth and holiness, mingle with the heavenly throng and join their songs of praise? Could they endure the glory of God and the Lamb?

No, no; they have never trained the mind to love purity; they have never learned the language of heaven, and now it is too late. A life of rebellion against God has unfitted them for heaven. Its purity, holiness, and peace would be torture to them; the glory of God would be a consuming fire. They would long to flee from that holy place. They would welcome destruction, that they might be hidden from the face of Him who died to redeem them. The destiny of the wicked is fixed by their own choice. Their exclusion from heaven is voluntary with themselves, and just and merciful on the part of God.

Like the waters of the Flood, the fires of the great day declare

God's verdict that the wicked are incurable. They have no disposition to submit to divine authority. Their will has been exercised in revolt; and when life is ended, it is too late to turn the current of their thoughts in the opposite direction, too late to turn from transgression to obedience, from hatred to love.

Final Thought

According to the Bible, and frankly common sense, only those who love God and surrender themselves to His Word will be content to be in heaven. After all, if someone hated God here on earth and His way of doing things, how could they possibly be happy when they were in heaven? It would be culture shock!

Can you imagine a thief who never surrendered his or her will to God? Imagine that person strolling around heaven's streets of gold. That thief would be hard pressed not to take a jackhammer to the road and hoard all that gold for himself! The problem of sin would never be laid to rest.

So from this chapter, we've learned that people who died in their sins won't automatically go to heaven, but we've also learned that they won't go to hell to suffer for all ages. So what happens to them when they die?

19

Why Evil Was Spared

Many U.S. Presidents have left a trail of controversial pardons and commuted sentences in their wake. On his first full day in office in 1977, President Jimmy Carter granted blanket amnesty to thousands of draft resisters from the Vietnam War. While his action was seen as courageous by some, many veterans considered it traitorous.

The most controversial pardon was probably President Gerald Ford's absolution of Nixon in 1974, assuring that the former president would not face criminal charges over the Watergate scandal. The action caused an enormous backlash that many believe cost Ford the 1976 election.

Former President Bill Clinton pardoned or commuted the prison sentences of 176 people on his last day in office. Pardon recipients included an accused tax swindler who was the former husband of a major Clinton donor, two felons who paid Clinton's brother-in-law $400,000 to lobby on their behalf, and the former president's own half-brother.

The idea of giving pardons and/or commuting sentences is nothing new, of course. Whether deserved or undeserved, the practice stretches back over the centuries, to the very beginning of this world.

Cain's murder of Abel is one of the more revolting stories in the Bible. Abel, who was in the prime of his life and one of the joys of Adam and Eve's lives, did nothing more than try to serve God correctly. For this he was attacked and murdered by his brother.

God could have sent Cain to the "electric chair" immediately, and most people would have considered it a just sentence. But God didn't. The Bible doesn't tell us that Cain ever truly repented of his sin, or even said he was sorry. Instead, we are told that he and his descendants became more and more wicked.

So it's hard to imagine that Cain ever asked for—or received—forgiveness or a pardon from God for that murder. But God did commute Cain's sentence. Instead of punishing Cain immediately, God allowed the murderer to live on for many more years on this earth.

Why Cain Was Allowed to Live

In sparing the life of Cain the murderer, God gave the world an example of what would be the result of permitting the sinner to continue a course of unbridled iniquity. Through the influence of Cain's teaching and example, multitudes of his descendants were led into sin, until "the wickedness of man was great in the earth" and "every imagination of the thoughts of his heart was only evil continually. . . . The earth also was corrupt before God, and the earth was filled with violence" (Genesis 6:5, 11).

In mercy to the world, God blotted out the wicked people of Noah's time. In mercy He destroyed the corrupt dwellers in Sodom.

Satan loves to deceive people into feeling sympathetic with those who do wrong, and even to admire them. In this way, the wicked are able to constantly lead others into rebellion. It was so in Cain's and in Noah's day, it was so in the time of Abraham and Lot; and it is so in our time. When God does finally destroy the rejecters of His grace, it will actually be an act of mercy to the universe—since such wayward ones will no longer be able to lead others to ruin and destruction.

"The wages of sin is death; but the gift of God is eternal life through Jesus Christ our Lord" (Romans 6:23). While life is the inheritance of the righteous, death is the portion of the wicked. Moses declared to Israel, "I have set before thee this day life and good, and death and evil" (Deuteronomy 30:15). The death referred to in these scriptures is not that pronounced upon Adam, for all mankind suffer the penalty of his transgression. It is "the second death" that is placed in contrast with everlasting life.

Because of Adam's sin, death became the lot of the entire human race. All alike go down into the grave. And through the provisions of the plan of salvation, all are to be brought forth from their graves. "There shall be a resurrection of the dead, both of the just and unjust" (Acts 24:15); "for as in Adam all die, even so in Christ shall all be made alive" (1 Corinthians 15:22).

A distinction is made, however, between the two classes that are brought forth. "All that are in the graves shall hear His voice, and shall come forth; they that have done good, unto the resurrection of life; and they that have done evil, unto the resurrection of damnation" (John 5:28, 29). They who have been "accounted worthy" of the resurrection of life are "blessed and holy." "On such the second death hath no power" (Revelation 20:6).

But those who have not, through repentance and faith, secured pardon, must receive the penalty of transgression—"the wages of sin." They suffer punishment varying in duration and intensity, "according to their works," but finally ending in the second death.

Since it is impossible for God, consistently with His justice and mercy, to save the sinner in his sins, He deprives him of the existence that his transgressions have forfeited and of which he has proved himself unworthy. Says an inspired writer, "Yet a little while, and the wicked shall not be: yea, thou shalt diligently consider his place, and it shall not be" (Psalm 37:10). And another declares, "They shall be as though they had not been" (Obadiah 16). Covered with infamy, they sink into hopeless, eternal oblivion.

At this point in the history of the universe, sin—and all the woe and ruin that have resulted from it—will be no more. In the words of the psalmist, "Thou hast destroyed the wicked, Thou hast put out their name forever and ever. O thou enemy, destructions are come to a perpetual end" (Psalm 9:5, 6).

The apostle John looked forward to this eternal order of things in the book of Revelation, when he heard a universal anthem of praise that included not one single note of discord. Every creature in heaven and earth was heard praising and giving glory to God (Revelation 5:13).

Final Thought

The story of Cain is not much different than the devil's. God refused to immediately destroy the devil because He wanted the world to know the painful path of rebellion. Likewise, God spared Cain so the world could see what evils would happen if just one person turned against Him.

This story is also important because we learn that God is patient even with humans, waiting and waiting for them to turn from evil and submit to Him. He doesn't desire to destroy us, but to forgive and grant eternal life.

We should never have the attitude that we will be okay with just a little sin—a little evil here and there. The Bible says that the wages of sin, any rebellion, is death. Those who surrender their sins to God will enjoy heaven, while those who don't will face something far different. So surrender your heart to God . . . and do it today.

20

The Truth About Death

There's an old story about Ethan Allen, the Revolutionary War hero. Allen was courting a young widow and each evening, in order to make it home faster after spending time with his beloved, he took a shortcut through the local cemetery. Some of Allen's pious New England neighbors noticed his practice and, feeling he was a bit irreverent, conspired to teach him a lesson.

Having noticed that Allen vaulted over the cemetery's cobblestone wall at exactly the same place each evening, they dug a grave in that very spot. That evening, when Allen nimbly cleared the cemetery wall, he landed in a heap at the bottom of the excavation. Unharmed, Allen quickly regained his footing and was preparing to climb out of the grave, when suddenly a ghostly figure draped in a white sheet peered down at him.

"Ethan Allen," it asked in a sepulchral voice, "what are thou doing in my grave?"

With a trace of irritation, Allen retorted, "Sir, that is not the question! The question is: What in thunder art thou doing out of it?"

Smile as we may at this little story, there is more than a grain of truth to it. If the spirits of our dead loved ones are indeed in the world all around us—as many churches teach—what are these people doing out of their graves? Is this biblical? Is this what Jesus, the apostles, and the early church fathers taught?

Everything we've talked about in this book so far culminates right here. It's time to discover what exactly happened to Katie when she died.

The doctrine taught by many churches, that people are conscious in death, is opposed to teachings of the Scripture, the dictates of reason, and our own feelings of humanity.

The popular belief today is that the redeemed in heaven are watching everything that takes place on earth—especially the lives of friends they have left behind. But how could the dead be happy if they know the troubles of the living, witness the sins committed by their own loved ones, or see them enduring all the sorrows, disappointments, and anguish of life?

How much of heaven's bliss would be enjoyed by those who were hovering over their friends on earth? And how utterly revolting is the belief that as soon as the breath leaves the body the soul of the impenitent is consigned to the flames of hell! To what depths of anguish must those be plunged who see their friends passing to the grave unprepared, to enter upon an eternity of woe and sin! Many have been driven to insanity by this harrowing thought.

What Does the Bible Say?

In the Psalms, David declares that man is not conscious in death. "His breath goeth forth, he returneth to his earth; in that very day his thoughts perish" (Psalm 146:4).

Solomon bears the same testimony: "The living know that they shall die: but the dead know not anything. . . . Their love, and their hatred, and their envy, is now perished; neither have they any more a portion forever in anything that is done under the sun. . . . There is no work, nor device, nor knowledge, nor wisdom, in the grave, whither thou goest" (Ecclesiastes 9:5, 6, 10).

When Hezekiah's life was prolonged for 15 years in answer to his prayer, the grateful king praised God for His great mercy with a song that tells why he was rejoicing: "The grave cannot praise Thee, death cannot celebrate Thee: they that go down into the pit cannot hope for Thy truth. The living, the living, he shall praise Thee, as I do this day" (Isaiah 38:18, 19).

Popular theology represents the righteous dead as in heaven, entered into bliss and praising God with an immortal tongue; but Hezekiah could see no such glorious prospect in death. His words agree with the testimony of the psalmist: "In death there is no remembrance of Thee: in the grave who shall give Thee thanks?"

(Psalms 6:5). "The dead praise not the Lord, neither any that go down into silence" (Psalms 115:17).

On the Day of Pentecost, Peter declared that the patriarch David "is both dead and buried, and his sepulcher is with us unto this day. . . . For David is not ascended into the heavens" (Acts 2:29, 34). The fact that David remains in the grave until the resurrection proves that the righteous do not go to heaven at death. It is only through the resurrection, and by virtue of the fact that Christ has risen, that David can at last sit at the right hand of God.

In the words of the apostle Paul, "If the dead rise not, then is not Christ raised: and if Christ be not raised, your faith is vain; ye are yet in your sins. Then they also which are fallen asleep in Christ are perished" (1 Corinthians 15:16-18).

If for 4,000 years the righteous had gone directly to heaven at death, how could Paul have said that if there is no resurrection, "they also which are fallen asleep in Christ are perished?" If the righteous are already in heaven, and the wicked go straight to hell, no resurrection would be necessary.

Many Christians believe that the church's most respected and revered fathers supported the idea of an immortal soul and eternally burning hell. This is not the case, however. By a vast majority, the early church leaders believed the plainest readings of Scripture.

Early Church Teachings

The martyr Tyndale, referring to the state of the dead, declared: "I confess openly, that I am not persuaded that they be already in the full glory that Christ is in, or the elect angels of God are in. Neither is it any article of my faith; for if it were so, I see not but then the preaching of the resurrection of the flesh were a thing in vain" (William Tyndale, *Preface to New Testament* [ed. 1534]. Reprinted in *British Reformers*—Tindal, Frith, Barnes, page 349).

It is an undeniable fact that the hope of immortal bliss at death has led to a widespread neglect of the Bible doctrine of the resurrection. This tendency was noted by Dr. Adam Clarke, who said, "The doctrine of the resurrection appears to have been thought of much more consequence among the primitive Christians than it is now! How is this? The apostles were continually insisting on it, and exciting the followers of God to diligence, obedience, and cheerfulness through it. And their successors in the present day seldom mention it! So apostles preached, and so primitive Christians believed; so we preach, and so our hearers believe. There is not a doctrine in the gospel on which more stress is laid; and there is not a doctrine in the present system of preaching which is treated with more neglect!" (*Commentary*, remarks on I Corinthians 15, paragraph 3).

Unfortunately, this line of thinking has continued until the glorious truth of the resurrection has been almost wholly lost sight of by the Christian world. Thus a leading religious writer, commenting on the words of Paul in 1 Thessalonians 4:13-18, says, "For all practical purposes of comfort the doctrine of the blessed immortality of the righteous takes the place for us of any doubtful doctrine of the Lord's second coming. At our death the Lord comes for us. That is what we are to wait and watch for. The dead are already passed into glory. They do not wait for the trump for their judgment and blessedness."

What Jesus Said

When about to leave His disciples, Jesus did not tell them that they would soon come to Him. "I go to prepare a place for you," He said. "And if I go and prepare a place for you, I will come again, and receive you unto Myself" (John 14:2, 3). And Paul tells us, further, that "the Lord Himself shall descend from heaven with a shout, with the voice of the Archangel, and with the trump of God: and the dead in Christ shall rise first: then we which are alive and remain shall be caught up together with them in the clouds, to meet the Lord in the air: and so shall we ever be with the Lord." And he adds, "Comfort one another with these words" (1 Thessalonians 4:16-18).

How wide the contrast between these words of comfort and those we so often hear today! Many console their bereaved friends with the assurance that, however sinful the deceased might have been, he or she went to live with the angels immediately after the last breath. In contrast, Paul points his brethren to the future coming of the Lord, when the fetters of the tomb shall be broken, and the "dead in Christ" shall be raised to eternal life.

Consider for a moment the little girl who Jesus raised from the dead. Most people, including pastors, will tell you that the moment she died, her soul went to be with God in paradise. Already in the most unimaginable bliss, experiencing the joys of heaven, Jesus calls her back to life and she is suddenly back on earth, full of sin and disease. The same thing happened to Jesus' friend Lazarus. Yet having experienced what every person seeks to understand, we don't hear a word about heaven from them. Here's a chance for the Bible writers to make heaven really come alive, and nothing is mentioned except that both need help. Does that make sense to you?

Is There Reward and Punishment Before Judgment?

Before any can enter the mansions of heaven, their cases must be investigated by God. Their characters and deeds must pass in review before the great judge of the universe. All are to be judged according to the things written in the books, and all will be rewarded according to their works.

This judgment does not take place at death. In the words of Paul: "He hath appointed a day, in the which He will judge the world in righteousness by that Man whom He hath ordained; whereof He hath given assurance unto all men, in that He hath raised Him from the dead" (Acts 17:31). Here the apostle plainly stated that a specified time, then future, had been fixed upon for the judgment of the world.

Jude refers to the same period: "The angels which kept not their first estate, but left their own habitation, He hath reserved in everlasting chains under darkness unto the judgment of the great day." And, again, he quotes the words of Enoch: "Behold, the Lord cometh with ten thousands of His saints, to execute judgment upon all" (Jude 6, 14, 15). John declares that he "saw the dead, small and great, stand before God; and the books were opened: . . . and the dead were judged out of those things which were written in the books" (Revelation 20:12).

But if the dead are already enjoying the bliss of heaven or writhing in the flames of hell, why do we need a future judgment? The teachings of God's Word on these important points are neither obscure nor contradictory; they may be understood by common minds. But what candid mind can see either wisdom or justice in the current theory? Will the righteous, after the investigation of their cases at the judgment, receive the commendation, "Well done, thou good and faithful servant ... *enter thou* into the joy of thy Lord," when they have been dwelling in His presence, perhaps for long ages (Matthew 25:21)?

Are the wicked summoned from the place of torment to receive sentence from the Judge of all the earth: "Depart from Me, ye cursed, into everlasting fire" (Matthew 25:41)? Oh, solemn mockery! shameful impeachment of the wisdom and justice of God!

The Case Is Closed

The theory of the immortality of the soul was one of the false doctrines that Rome, borrowing from paganism, incorporated into the religion of Christendom.

Martin Luther classed it with the "monstrous fables that form part of the Roman dunghill of decretals" (E. Petavel, *The Problem of Immortality*, page 255). Commenting on the words of Solomon in Ecclesiastes, that the dead know not anything, the Reformer says, "Another place proving that the dead have no ... feeling. There is, saith he, no duty, no science, no knowledge, no wisdom there. Solomon judgeth that the dead are asleep, and feel nothing at all. For the dead lie there, accounting neither days nor years, but when they are awaked, they shall seem to have slept scarce one minute" (Martin Luther, *Exposition of Solomon's Booke Called Ecclesiastes*, page 152).

Nowhere in the Sacred Scriptures is found the statement that the righteous go to their reward or the wicked to their punishment at death. The patriarchs and prophets have left no such assurance. Christ and His apostles have given no hint of it. The Bible clearly teaches that the dead do not go immediately to heaven. They are represented as sleeping until the resurrection (1 Thessalonians 4:14; Job 14:10-12).

In the very day when the silver cord is loosed and the golden bowl broken (Ecclesiastes 12:6), man's thoughts perish. They that go down to the grave are in silence. They know no more of anything that is done under the sun (Job 14:21).

This is a blessed rest for the weary righteous! Time, be it long or short, is but a moment to them. They sleep; they are awakened by the trump of God to a glorious immortality. "For the trumpet shall sound, and the dead shall be raised incorruptible. . . . So when this corruptible shall have put on incorruption, and this mortal shall have put on immortality, then shall be brought to pass the saying that is written, Death is swallowed up in victory" (1 Corinthians 15:52-54).

As they are called forth from their deep slumber they begin to think just where they ceased. The last sensation was the pang of death; the last thought, that they were falling beneath the power of the grave. When they arise from the tomb, their first glad thought will be echoed in the triumphal shout, "O death, where is thy sting? O grave, where is thy victory?" (v. 55).

For many, this is a stunning revelation. In fact, you might be sad or upset, or even angry, but I want you to put that aside for a moment and consider closely everything you've just read. In fact, perhaps you should read this chapter again and try to take in even more information.

Remember, the devil knows that this topic is an emotional one, and he wants to do everything to take your eyes away from what God says and present you a picture he says is better. Don't fall for that; let's stick with the Bible. Indeed, take out your Bible and open its pages as you read this chapter again. Look at every Bible verse listed and see if what you read really fits the Bible.

According to the Bible then, Katie is "sleeping in her grave." When her life was taken that day on that motorcycle, as cold as it might sound, her consciousness ended. She's not with grandma in heaven, like the pastor said. And though that might sound sad and terrible, I want you to go one step further with me so you can know why the truth about our departed loved ones is so reassuring, and so necessary to know.

If according to the Bible the "spirit" that contacted the Fox sisters through the rapping wasn't a person from beyond the grave, what else could it be? If they weren't making up the episode, what or who did they hear and communicate with, and how could it know where and why those bones turned up in their house?

With the Fox sisters' dramatic rise in wealth and riches and their subsequent collapse into poverty, alcoholism, and controversy, what do you think really happened? We're about to find out.

Final Thought

Before you go on to the next chapter, I want to ask you, "Are you upset or angry with what you have read?" Think about it for a minute and then ask yourself "Why?"

I was angry when I first learned the truth too, but I wonder if it was for the same reason. When I surrendered my heart to Christ, I knew that I must accept His truths in His way. He's looking out for us, and He would never lie . . . giving Him the benefit of the doubt makes the most sense.

But as a matter of fact, I got angry because when I learned the truth, I realized that all those things I had been taught that the Bible says about death were obviously very wrong. It upset me that I misjudged God all that time, because I hadn't looked at it closely enough myself.

I'm not angry anymore. Indeed, with this truth, I am full of joy and assurance that God is in control and is very, very good to His creation. I am so glad for a foundation that is sure.

21

The Lurking Danger

Without question, interest in the supernatural has exploded all over America. Whether the cause is simple curiosity or full-blown religious belief, people are exploring the paranormal with renewed enthusiasm. It seems that popular entertainment has taken its cue from culture, fanning interest in the supernatural with films, books, magazines, television shows, and psychic telephone hotlines.

The most wildly popular book in recent years has been the *Harry Potter* witchcraft series by author J.K. Rowling, who, thanks to her success as a writer, is now the richest woman in England. Although written for children, the books also appeal strongly to adults. Rowling's books show the maturing Potter casting spells and dealing with the spirits of the dead to achieve his goals. Books in the *Harry Potter* series also lambaste those who deny the reality of witchcraft or consider the practice evil, such as Potter's cruel guardians.

Hollywood is also profiting from the culture's interest in the paranormal. In the past few years, the number of horror and spiritualistic productions generated by the "entertainment capital of the world" has increased dramatically.

One of the most popular productions was *The Sixth Sense,* about a young boy who can see and communicate with the dead. Ghost stories, such as *The Mothman Prophecies* and *Dragonfly,* also continue to abound. These slick productions draw in viewers with eye-popping special effects and classy Hollywood treatment.

Yet without a doubt, the most influential media resides in the home—television. From the heroine show *Buffy the Vampire Slayer* to *The X-Files,* prime time television is awash in spiritualistic programming.

Although the skeptical-minded FBI agent Scully in *The X-Files* has a strong Catholic belief and decries most of the opinions of her partner's conspiracy-minded alien ideas, she believes in a ghostly afterlife herself. Ironically, Scully's alien-minded partner flatly rejects those ideas.

The show *Medium* features a woman who is able to channel the dead to solve crimes. Of course, even at the dawn of television, witchcraft was shown in a positive light with *Bewitched,* which has also been revived in Hollywood with A-list stars Nicole Kidman and Will Ferrell.

Have you ever stopped to wonder why all this is happening now? Why are TV shows, movies, books, and video games now featuring spiritualism—once considered an anathema to the Christian faith—quickly becoming a large part of the average Christian's viewing diet? Is this just Christianity growing up, or does it mean something else, especially in the light of what we've learned so far?

Although the popular acceptance of the spirit world within the Christian church is relatively new, the rise of mediums and other spiritualistic practices within the framework of Christianity can be seen in such shows as *Crossing Over,* hosted by medium John Edward. Edward claims to have the power to speak with the dead, and now he has written a book called *Practical Praying: Using the Rosary to Enhance Your Life* that intermingles Christian heroes with New Age spiritualism. The questions is, if he really believes in the power of the Christian faith, why does he do something the Bible expressly forbids and teach something that the Bible does not?

Furthermore, one of the most successful religious-themed television shows ever was *Touched by an Angel,* which featured a mix of angels and the spirits of the dead helping humans on earth. More recently, the NBC hit miniseries *Revelations* incorporated interest in the end-time Armageddon and contact with spirits beyond the grave for a strange buffet of Christian doctrines and spiritualism.

Why is all this happening? If you remember, not long after Katie died, a mysterious person called her parents to say she had direct contact with their little girl from beyond the grave. Yet while the Bible says that communicating with the dead is not even possible, millions of people, even Christians, are beginning to see things differently.

So what exactly is going on?

22

An Age of Confusion

In case you've missed it, major apparitions of the Virgin Mary are increasing every year and all over the world. Since the first recorded supernatural appearance of Mary to a third-century lawyer, thousands of apparitions of the Virgin have been claimed. Moreover, hundreds of visions have been reported in the twentieth century alone, although only a few have ever received official "approval" by the Catholic Church.

The December 30, 1991 issue of *Time* magazine reported that "the late 20th century has become the age of the Marian pilgrimage" to many shrines established to commemorate the many sightings of the Virgin Mary in recent years. Perhaps the two most famous shrines are at Lourdes, France, and Fatima, Portugal. But "there are thousands of shrines of Our Lady in every country of the world" (*Shrines to our Lady,* p. V).

Shrines are usually built at locations where an apparition has appeared. Especially in the twentieth century, Mary apparitions have been reported and shrines erected in Portugal, Ireland, Rwanda, Venezuela, Italy, Yugoslavia, Korea, Mexico, Japan, and many other countries—drawing millions of visitors every year.

I might sound like a broken record, but what is going on in light of the clear teaching of the Bible? Is Mary the mother of Jesus really appearing with increasing frequency around the world? The Bible says many times that Jesus will come again, but it never makes any such promise about Mary. Is an angel behind these apparitions? Is it Mary? Or is it the working of some other power?

The working of holy angels, as presented in the Bible, is a very comforting and precious truth to every follower of Christ. Unfortunately, the Bible teachings about angels have been obscured by the errors of popular theology. The idea that people are naturally immortal, which was borrowed from pagan philosophy during the darkness of the great apostasy and incorporated into the Christian faith, has pushed out the truth so plainly taught in Scripture—that "the dead know not anything" (Ecclesiastes 9:5).

Millions have come to believe that it is spirits of the dead who are the "ministering spirits, sent forth to minister for them who shall be heirs of salvation" (Hebrews 1:14). And they believe this wholeheartedly, despite the testimony of Scripture to the existence of heavenly angels and their connection with the history of man before a human being had even died.

The doctrine of man's consciousness in death, especially the belief that spirits of the dead return to minister to the living, has prepared the way for modern spiritualism. If the dead enter the presence of God and holy angels, and are blessed with knowledge far exceeding what they had before, why should they not return to the earth to enlighten and instruct the living?

If, as taught by popular theologians, spirits of the dead are hovering about their friends on earth, why should they not be permitted to communicate with them, to warn them against evil or to comfort them in sorrow? How can those who believe in man's consciousness in death reject what comes to them as divine light communicated by glorified spirits?

This channel, which is regarded as sacred by many Christians, is one of Satan's prime tools for the accomplishment of his purposes. Fallen angels who do Satan's bidding appear as messengers from the spirit world. Under the guise of bringing the living into communication with the dead, the prince of evil exercises his bewitching influence upon human minds. He has power to bring what looks like departed friends before men.

The counterfeit is perfect: The familiar look, the words, the tone, are reproduced with marvelous distinctness. Many are comforted with the assurance that their loved ones are enjoying the bliss of heaven, and without suspicion of danger, they give ear "to seducing spirits, and doctrines of devils" (1 Timothy 4:1).

Once Satan has convinced people that the dead actually

do return to communicate with them, his next step is to "bring up" those who went to Christ-less graves. These people then claim to be happy in heaven, and even to occupy exalted positions there. In this way, he is able to spread widely the error that there is no difference in the eternal destination of the righteous and the wicked.

These pretended visitors from the spirit world utter cautions and warnings that sometimes turn out to be correct. Then, as confidence is gained, they present doctrines that directly undermine faith in the Bible. While pretending to have the deepest interest in the well-being of their friends on earth, they insinuate the most dangerous errors. The fact that they state some truths, and are able at times to foretell future events, gives their statements an appearance of reliability. As a result, their false teachings are accepted by many as readily, and believed as implicitly, as if they were the most sacred truths of the Bible. The law of God is set aside, the Spirit of grace despised, the blood of the covenant counted an unholy thing. The spirits deny the deity of Christ and place even the Creator on a level with themselves. In this way, and under a new disguise, the great rebel still carries on his warfare against God, begun in heaven and continued on earth for nearly 6,000 years.

Many people try to explain these supernatural occurrences as a fraud or sleight of hand on the part of the medium. But while the results of trickery have often been palmed off as genuine manifestations, there have also been marked exhibitions of supernatural power.

The mysterious rapping with which modern spiritualism began was not the result of human trickery or cunning. It was the direct work of evil angels who, through rapping, introduced one of the most successful of soul-destroying delusions. Many will be ensnared through the belief that spiritualism is mere human trickery. Then when brought face to face with events that are undeniably supernatural, they will be deceived and led to accept them as the great power of God.

These persons overlook what the Bible says about the wonders wrought by Satan and his agents. It was by satanic aid that Pharaoh's magicians were able to counterfeit the work of God. Paul testifies that before the second advent of Christ, there will be similar manifestations of satanic power. The coming of the Lord is to be preceded by "the working of Satan with all power and signs and lying wonders, and with all deceivableness of unrighteousness" (2 Thessalonians 2:9, 10).

The apostle John, describing the miracle-working power that will be manifested in the last days, declares, "He doeth great wonders, so that he maketh fire come down from heaven on the earth in the sight of men, and deceiveth them that dwell on the earth by the means of those miracles which he had power to do" (Revelation 13:13, 14). The Bible is not talking about mere imposters here. Men will be deceived by miracles that Satan's agents have power to do—not that they pretend to do.

The prince of darkness, who bent the powers of his mastermind toward the work of deception for thousands of years, skillfully adapts his temptations to men of all classes and conditions. To persons of culture and refinement, he presents spiritualism in its more refined and intellectual aspect. In this way, he succeeds in drawing many into his snare.

The wisdom that spiritualism imparts is described by the apostle James as that which "descendeth not from above, but is earthly, sensual, devilish" (James 3:15). The devil is an expert at concealing this fact, however, when concealment will best suit his purpose.

He who could appear clothed with the brightness of the heavenly seraphs before Christ in the wilderness of temptation comes to men in the most attractive manner as an angel of light. He appeals to the reason by the presentation of elevating themes; he delights the fancy with enrapturing scenes; and he enlists the affections by his eloquent portrayals of love and charity.

He excites the imagination to lofty flights, leading men to take such great pride in their own wisdom that, in their hearts, they despise the Eternal One. That mighty being who could take the world's Redeemer to an exceedingly high mountain and bring before Him all the kingdoms of the earth and the glory of them, will present his temptations to men in a manner to pervert the senses of all who are not shielded by divine power.

Final Thought

Just like God has His master plan for you and this world, Satan has his. He's doing everything in his power, from trickery to bribery, to get you and others to accept his way and thus reject God. He wants you to go to hell; it's as simple as that.

And that's why it is so important to realize that we are part of a dangerous battle between good and evil. It is a controversy that has engrossed this planet since its creation, and it is eternally important that you know right from wrong.

Satan does not care how he deceives us. He will use to his advantage our sin-hungry senses—sight, touch, hearing, speaking, even smelling—for our ruin. He will maliciously resort to using your feelings about your dead loved ones to convince you to reject God's truth, speaking attractive half-lies.

That's why, in the beginning, I wrote about us reasoning together . . . about using more than feelings to determine truth. Satan wants to use your feelings against you. Don't let him . . . put your trust, reason, and feelings into the Word of God only.

23

Who or What Are
Mediums Contacting?

E manuel Swedenborg was a highly educated and well-respected
scientist and scholar known throughout Europe. Among other
accomplishments, Swedenborg sketched a flying machine, a
submarine, and a rapid-fire gun; wrote a book of poetry in Latin; and
published books on algebra.

Beginning in his fifties, though, Swedenborg claimed to have
mystical experiences. Swedenborg not only believed that he was in
constant communication with the dead, but he also said he was given
a tour of heaven and hell.

Swedenborg felt it was his duty to reveal to those on earth the
future existence awaiting them and to reveal the spiritual laws that
prevail in both this world and the next. His descriptions of the other
side were based on visits he had with various spirits and "voices" he
heard internally.

Yet Emanuel Swedenborg was not the first successful and
respected leader to consult with evil spirits. Indeed, communications
with the spirit world go back to Bible times. One of the saddest, and
for some, most difficult to understand stories about communicating
with the dead involves King Saul and the witch of Endor.

The Bible story of Saul's visit to the witch of Endor has been
a source of perplexity to many. While some Christians believe that
Samuel was actually present at the interview with Saul, the Bible
itself furnishes sufficient ground for a contrary conclusion.

If Samuel really was called out of heaven to meet with Saul,
he must have been "summoned down," either by the power of God

or Satan. None can believe for a moment that Satan had power to call the holy prophet of God from heaven to honor the incantations of an abandoned woman. Nor can we conclude that God summoned him to the witch's cave; for the Lord had already refused to communicate with Saul, by dreams, by Urim, or by prophets (1 Samuel 28:6). These were God's own appointed mediums of communication, and He did not pass them by to deliver the message through the agent of Satan.

The Message Reveals Its Origin

The message delivered to Saul by the witch of Endor is, itself, sufficient evidence of its origin. The words of the apparition were not designed to lead Saul to repentance, but rather, to urge him on to ruin. This is not the work of God, but of Satan. Furthermore, the act of Saul in consulting a sorceress is cited in Scripture as one reason why he was rejected by God and abandoned to destruction: "Saul died for his transgression which he committed against the Lord, even against the word of the Lord, which he kept not, and also for asking counsel of one that had a familiar spirit, to inquire of it; and inquired not of the Lord: therefore He slew him, and turned the kingdom unto David the son of Jesse" (1 Chronicles 10:13, 14). Here it is distinctly stated that Saul inquired of the familiar spirit, not of the Lord. He did not communicate with Samuel, the prophet of God; but through the sorceress he held intercourse with Satan. Satan could not present the real Samuel, but he did present a counterfeit, that served his purpose of deception.

Nearly all forms of ancient sorcery and witchcraft were founded upon a belief in communion with the dead. Those who practiced the arts of witchcraft claimed to converse with departed spirits, and to get knowledge of future events from them. This custom of consulting the dead is referred to in the prophecy of Isaiah: "When they shall say unto you, Seek unto them that have familiar spirits, and unto wizards that peep and that mutter: should not a people seek unto their God? for the living to the dead?" (Isaiah 8:19).

The Cornerstone of Idolatry

This same belief in communion with the dead was the cornerstone of heathen idolatry. The gods of the heathen were believed to be the deified spirits of departed heroes. The religion of heathen nations was really a worship of the dead. This is evident from the Scriptures. For example, in the account of the sin of Israel at Bethpeor, the Bible tells us that "Israel abode in Shittim, and the people began to commit whoredom with the daughters of Moab. And they called the people unto the sacrifices of their gods: and the people did eat, and bowed down to their gods. And Israel joined himself unto Baalpeor" (Numbers 25:1-3). The psalmist tells us to what kind of gods these sacrifices were offered. Speaking of the same apostasy of the Israelites, he says, "They joined themselves also unto Baalpeor, and ate the sacrifices of the dead" (Psalm 106:28); that is, sacrifices that had been offered to the dead.

The deification of the dead has held a prominent place in nearly every system of heathenism, as has also the supposed communion with the dead. The gods were believed to communicate their will to men, and also, when consulted, to give them counsel. These types of communications were where many of the famous oracles of Greece and Rome came from.

Even in professedly Christian lands, many still believe they can communicate with the dead. This practice has become particularly widespread, first under the name of spiritualism, and then the New Age movement. It is calculated to take hold of the sympathies of those who have laid their loved ones in the grave. Spiritual beings sometimes appear to persons in the form of their deceased friends, and relate incidents connected with their lives and perform acts which they performed while living. In this way they lead men to believe that their dead friends are angels, hovering over them and communicating with them. Those who thus assume to be the spirits of the departed are regarded with a certain idolatry, and with many their word has greater weight than the Word of God.

A Snare for the People of Israel

By predicting the doom of Saul, Satan planned to trick the people of Israel. He hoped that they would be inspired with confidence in the sorceress, and would be led to consult her. Then they would turn from God as their counselor, and place themselves under the guidance of Satan.

The lure by which spiritualism attracts millions is its pretended power to draw aside the veil from the future and reveal what God has hidden. God has opened before us the great events of the future. In His word, He has told us all that it is essential for us to know. In His word, He has given us a safe guide for our feet amid all of life's perils. It is Satan's purpose, however, to destroy men's confidence in God. The devil wants to make us dissatisfied with our condition in life, to lead us to seek a knowledge of what God has wisely veiled from us, and to despise what He has revealed in His Holy Word.

There are many who become restless when they cannot know the definite outcome of affairs. They can't endure uncertainty, and in their impatience they refuse to wait to see the salvation of God. The very apprehension of evil drives them nearly to distraction. They give way to their rebellious feelings, and run hither and thither in passionate grief, seeking intelligence concerning things that have not been revealed.

The Source of Divine Consolation

If they would but trust in God, and watch unto prayer, they would find divine consolation. Their spirit would be calmed by communion with God. The weary and the heavy-laden would find rest unto their souls if they would only go to Jesus; but when they neglect the means that God has ordained for their comfort, and resort to other sources, hoping to learn what God has withheld, they commit the error of Saul, and gain only a knowledge of evil.

God is not pleased when we consult with Satan, and He has expressed His displeasure in the most explicit terms. This impatient haste to tear away the veil from the future reveals a lack of faith in God and leaves the soul open to the suggestions of the master deceiver.

Satan leads men to consult the spirit world, and by revealing hidden things of the past, he inspires confidence in his power to foretell things to come. By experience gained through the long ages he can reason from cause to effect and often forecast, with a degree of accuracy, some of the future events of man's life. Thus he is enabled to deceive poor, misguided souls, bring them under his power and lead them captive at his will.

God has warned us through His prophet: "When they shall say unto you, Seek unto them that have familiar spirits, and unto wizards that peep and that mutter: should not a people seek unto their God? for the living to the dead? To the law and to the testimony: if they speak not according to this word, it is because there is no light in them" (Isaiah 8:19, 20).

Should Christians Consult the Devil?

Shall those who worship a holy God, infinite in wisdom and power, go to wizards, whose knowledge comes from intimacy with the enemy of our Lord? God Himself is the light of His people; He bids them fix their eyes by faith upon the glories that are veiled from human sight. The Sun of Righteousness sends its bright beams into their hearts; they have light from the throne of heaven, and they have no desire to turn away from the source of light to the messengers of Satan.

The demon's message to Saul, although including a denunciation of sin and a prophecy of retribution, was not meant to reform him, but to goad him to despair and ruin. Satan does not always use this tactic, however. Quite frequently it best serves the tempter's purpose to lure men to destruction by flattery.

The teaching of demon gods in ancient times promoted the vilest forms of sin. The divine law condemning sin and enforcing righteousness was set aside; truth was lightly regarded, and impurity was not only permitted but encouraged.

Spiritualism declares that there is no death, no sin, no judgment, no retribution; that "men are unfallen demigods;" that desire is the highest law; and that man is accountable only to himself. The barriers that God has erected to guard truth, purity, and reverence are broken down, and many are thus emboldened in sin. Does not such teaching suggest an origin similar to that of demon worship?

The Fruits of Demon Worship

God allowed the Israelites to see the results of holding communion with evil spirits in the abominations of the Canaanites, who were without natural affection, idolaters, adulterers, murderers, and abominable by every corrupt thought and revolting practice. Men do not know their own hearts; for "the heart is deceitful above all things, and desperately wicked" (Jeremiah 17:9).

God understands the tendencies of the depraved nature of man, however. Then, as now, Satan was watching to bring about conditions favorable to rebellion, that the people of Israel might make themselves as abhorrent to God as were the Canaanites.

The adversary of souls is ever on the alert to open channels for the unrestrained flow of evil in us; for he desires that we may be ruined, and be condemned before God.

Satan was determined to keep his hold on the land of Canaan, and when it became the home of the children of Israel, and the law of God was made the law of the land, the devil hated Israel with a cruel and malicious hatred. It was his constant work to plot the destruction of the people of God. Through the agency of evil spirits strange gods were introduced; and because of transgression, the chosen people were finally scattered from the Land of Promise.

This history Satan is striving to repeat in our day. God is leading His people out from the abominations of the world, that they may keep His law. Because of this, the rage of "the accuser of our brethren" knows no bounds. "The devil is come down unto you, having great wrath, because he knoweth that he hath but a short time" (Revelation 12:10, 12). The antitypical land of promise is just before us, and Satan is determined to destroy the people of God and cut them off from their inheritance. The admonition, "Watch ye and pray, lest ye enter into temptation" (Mark 14:38), was never more needed than now.

The word of the Lord to ancient Israel is addressed also to His people in this age: "Regard not them that have familiar spirits, neither seek after wizards, to be defiled by them;" "for all that do these things are an abomination unto the Lord" (Leviticus 19:31; Deuteronomy 18:12).

Final Thought

The devil knows our weaknesses. After all, he's had more than 6,000 years of experience getting to know what makes us stumble. He knows how much we miss those loved ones who have died, and how willing we are to hear some kind of good news about them. That means he also has the power to use them to trick you into forsaking God.

God, on the other hand, will use simple reason, truth, and love to earn your trust. While Satan is working to affect your emotions, making you trust in yourself and tickling your fancy, God wants your intellect and heart.

No matter how we want to slice it, pride and selfishness will ruin us. That's what the devil is betting on. Trust in God, believe what He says and the devil will lose the bet he's placed against you.

24

Satan
Versus God

In 1967, Nancy Reagan quietly but proudly stood by her husband Ronald as he was sworn into the office of the Governor of California—nine minutes after the time initially scheduled for the inauguration. The reason for the barely perceptible delay: According to Ronald Reagan's astrological star chart, 12:10 P.M. was the time most suited to ensure a good start and great success to his governorship.

It's common knowledge that the Reagans practiced a bizarre mix of reliance on the supernatural and Protestant Christianity throughout their political career. But did their interest in the paranormal affect the everyday world—your world?

On August 30, 1974, as Governor of California, Reagan signed legislation that enabled astrologers to legally practice their trade for money—by removing the profession from the negative categorization of "fortune teller." But even more than that, according to a former White House Chief of Staff, "Virtually every major move and decision the Reagans made during 1985-1987 was cleared in advance with a woman in San Francisco who drew up horoscopes to make certain that the planets were in a favorable alignment for the enterprise" (Ronald Reagan, *For the Record,* 1988).

What is most remarkable is not that an actor or even a powerful U.S. politician would consult the stars to determine policy, as Nixon and other well-known powerbrokers also dabbled in spiritualism, but rather the intense support of Christians for the Reagan presidency even after the astrology issue came to light. Historically, Christians, especially conservatives, have shunned what the Bible very clearly condemns: divination, speaking with the dead, fortune telling, etc. But as the response to Reagan and the quiet acceptance of spiritualism in America shows, all this is changing dramatically.

Satan used flattery to beguile Eve in the garden of Eden, and he is using the same tactic today. He loves to kindle a desire to obtain forbidden knowledge and excite ambition for self-exaltation in the hearts of men. These were the cherished evils that caused his fall, and through which he aims to accomplish the ruin of men.

"Ye shall be as gods," he declares, "knowing good and evil" (Genesis 3:5). Spiritualism teaches "that man is the creature of progression; that it is his destiny from his birth to progress, even to eternity, toward the Godhead." And again, "Each mind will judge itself and not another." "The judgment will be right, because it is the judgment of self . . . The throne is within you." In the words of one spiritualistic teacher, whose "spiritual consciousness" awoke within him, "My fellow men, all were unfallen demigods." Another declares, "Any just and perfect being is Christ."

Thus, in place of the righteousness and perfection of the infinite God, the true object of adoration; in place of the perfect righteousness of His law, the true standard of human attainment, Satan has substituted the sinful, erring nature of man himself as the only object of adoration, the only rule of judgment, or standard of character. The progress accomplished by such teachings is not upward, but downward.

One of the laws of both intellectual and spiritual nature is that by beholding we become changed. The mind gradually adapts itself to the subjects upon which it is allowed to dwell. It comes into harmony with what it loves and gives reverence to. Man will never rise higher than his own standard of purity or goodness or truth. If self is his loftiest ideal, he will never attain to anything more exalted. Rather, he will constantly sink lower and lower. The grace of God alone has power to exalt man. Left to himself, his course must inevitably be downward.

To the self-indulgent, the pleasure-loving and sensual, spiritualism presents itself under a less subtle disguise than to the more refined and intellectual. In the grosser forms of spiritualism, they find beliefs and practices that are in harmony with their natural inclinations.

Satan studies every indication of human frailty. He marks the sins that each individual is inclined to commit. Then he ensures that opportunities to gratify the tendency to evil will not be lacking.

Satan tempts men to overindulge in things that are of themselves lawful. Through intemperance, he causes men and women to weaken physical, mental, and moral power. He has destroyed and is destroying thousands through the indulgence of passion, thus brutalizing the entire nature of man.

Then to complete his diabolical work, he declares through spirits that "true knowledge places man above all law;" that "whatever is, is right;" that "God doth not condemn;" and that "all sins which are committed are innocent."

As people are thus led to believe that desire is the highest law, that liberty is license, and that man is accountable only to himself, is it any wonder that corruption and depravity thrive on every hand? Millions of people eagerly accept teachings that leave them at liberty to obey the promptings of the carnal heart. The reins of self-control are laid on the neck of lust, the powers of mind and soul are made subject to the animal propensities, and Satan exultingly sweeps thousands into his net who call themselves Christians.

What the Bible Teaches

No one needs to be deceived by the lying claims of spiritualism. God has given the world enough light to help them discover the snare. As we have already shown, the theory forming the very foundation of spiritualism is at war with the plainest statements of Scripture. The Bible declares that the dead know not anything, that their thoughts have perished; they have no part in anything that is done under the sun; they know nothing of the joys or sorrows of those who were dearest to them on earth.

Furthermore, God has expressly forbidden all pretended communication with departed spirits. In the days of the Hebrews, there was a class of people who claimed, as do the spiritualists of today, to hold communication with the dead. But the "familiar spirits," as these visitants from other worlds were called, are declared by the Bible to be "the spirits of devils." (Compare Numbers 25:1-3; Psalm 106:28; 1 Corinthians 10:20; Revelation 16:14.) The work of dealing with familiar spirits was pronounced an abomination to the

Lord, and was solemnly forbidden under penalty of death (Leviticus 19:31; 20:27).

Some people hold the very word "witchcraft" in contempt, believing that the claim of men to communicate with evil spirits is as a fable of the Dark Ages. But spiritualism, which numbers its converts by the millions, which has made its way into scientific circles, which has invaded churches, and has found favor in legislative bodies, and even in the courts of kings—this mammoth deception is but a revival, in a new disguise, of the witchcraft condemned and prohibited in the Bible.

If there were no other evidence of the real character of spiritualism, it should be enough for Christians to understand that spirits make no distinction between righteousness and sin, between the noblest and purest of the apostles of Christ and the most corrupt of the servants of Satan.

By representing the basest of men as in heaven, and highly exalted there, Satan says to the world, "No matter how wicked you are; no matter whether you believe or disbelieve God and the Bible. Live as you please; heaven is your home." The spiritualist teachers virtually declare, "Everyone that doeth evil is good in the sight of the Lord, and He delighteth in them; or, Where is the God of judgment?" (Malachi 2:17). Saith the Word of God, "Woe unto them that call evil good, and good evil; that put darkness for light, and light for darkness" (Isaiah 5:20).

By denying the divine origin of the Bible, spiritualists tear away the foundation of the Christian's hope, putting out the light that reveals the way to heaven. Satan is deceiving the world into believing that the Bible is mere fiction, or at least a book suited to the infancy of the race, but now to be lightly regarded or cast aside as obsolete.

To take the place of the Word of God, then Satan holds out spiritual manifestations. This channel is completely under his control. By making his demons appear as angels, he can lead the world to believe whatever he wants them to.

The Bible—the book that will judge the devil and his followers—is just where he wants it. The Savior of the world, Satan makes to be no more than a common man. Just as the Roman soldiers who guarded the tomb of Jesus spread a lying report to try and disprove the resurrection, spiritualist believers today try to make it appear that there is nothing miraculous in our Savior's life. After attempting to push Jesus into the background, they then call attention to their own miracles, declaring that they far exceed the works of Christ.

The NBC show *Revelations* is the epitome of spiritualism made to please and influence Christians, as a coma patient is used by the spirit of a dead girl to help her father fight the devil and prevent the oncoming Armageddon. The miniseries was one of the most successful broadcasts for the then-struggling broadcasting giant, indicating that anything to do with the paranormal, no matter how false, is a huge attraction to the average American family.

Spiritualism is, at this very moment, changing its form, veiling some of its more objectionable features, and assuming a Christian guise. The teachings of spiritualism have been stated plainly from both the platform and the press for many years; however, and in these statements, its real character stands revealed.

While spiritualism formerly denounced Christ and the Bible, it now professes to accept both. The Bible, however, is interpreted in a manner that is pleasing to the unrenewed heart, while its solemn and vital truths are made of no effect.

Love is dwelt upon as the chief attribute of God, but it is degraded to a weak and very sentimental feeling. Meanwhile, very little distinction is made between good and evil. God's justice, His denunciations of sin, and the requirements of His holy law are all kept out of sight.

People are taught to regard the Decalogue as a dead letter. Pleasing, bewitching fables captivate the senses and lead men to reject the Bible as the foundation of their faith. Christ is as verily denied as before; but Satan has so blinded the eyes of the people that the deception is not discerned.

There are few who have any real conception of the deceptive power of spiritualism and the danger of coming under its influence. Many tamper with it merely to gratify their curiosity. They have no real faith in it and would be filled with horror at the thought of yielding themselves to the spirits' control. But they venture upon the forbidden ground, and the mighty destroyer exercises his power upon them against their will.

Let them once be induced to submit their minds to his direction, and he holds them captive. It is impossible, in their own strength, to break away from the bewitching, alluring spell. Nothing but the power of God, granted in answer to the earnest prayer of faith, can deliver these ensnared souls.

Falling For Deceit

All who indulge sinful traits of character, or willfully cherish a known sin, are inviting the temptations of Satan. They separate themselves from God and the watchful care of His angels. Then, as the evil one presents his deceptions, they are without defense and fall an easy prey. Those who thus place themselves in Satan's power have little understanding of where their course will end. Once the devil has achieved the overthrow of these individuals, he uses them as his agents to lure others to ruin.

Says the prophet Isaiah: "When they shall say unto you, Seek unto them that have familiar spirits, and unto wizards that peep, and that mutter: should not a people seek unto their God? for the living to the dead? To the law and to the testimony: if they speak not according to this word, it is because there is no light in them" (Isaiah 8:19, 20).

If men had been willing to receive the truth so plainly stated in the Scriptures concerning the nature of man and the state of the dead, they would see the working of Satan with power and signs and lying wonders in the claims and manifestations of spiritualism.

People don't want to yield the liberty so agreeable to the carnal heart, however. They don't want to renounce the sins they love. And so millions close their eyes to the light and walk straight into Satan's traps. Regardless of the warnings of the Bible, Satan weaves his snares about them, and they become his prey.

"Because they received not the love of the truth, that they might be saved," therefore, "God shall send them strong delusion, that they should believe a lie" (2 Thessalonians 2:10, 11).

Final Thought

Playing with fire will eventually get you burned. It might be fun and exciting to deal with dangerous things, but doing so can leave scars that will stay with you a lifetime.

You must trust in what God says, that those who have died are resting in their graves, waiting for the resurrection. If you are ever confronted with some kind of spirit . . . a ghost of a dead loved one . . . don't play around. Renounce what you see as a trick of the devil and give yourself over to the protection of God.

Don't find entertainment or advice by watching so-called mediums speaking to dead loved ones; if these demons have the power to imitate your dead loves ones, do they not have the power to convince you that following God is wrong?

Don't play with fire; you'll only get burned.

25

Taking a
Stand

J.K. Rowling claims that the idea for the *Harry Potter* books suddenly came to her one day in 1990 while riding on a train. "The character of Harry just strolled into my mind. . . . I really did feel he was someone who walked up and introduced himself to my mind's eye" (*Reuters*, July 17, 2000).

Does this mean that everything readers discover in her books is an act of great imagination? Hardly.

If Rowling is not a practicing witch, she has studied deeply into the most detailed witchcraft training manuals—and she is pouring as much as she can into her ongoing series of books. Indeed, *Harry Potter* is a training book itself, as almost nothing about witchcraft is omitted!

According to some of Rowling's childhood friends, one of her favorite things to do as a child was to dress up as a witch. "We used to dress up and play Witch all the time. My brother would dress up as a wizard. Joanne was always reading witchcraft stories to us. . . . We would make secret potions for her. She would always send us off to get twigs for the potions" (Ian Potter and Vikki Potter, quoted in Danielle Demetriou's "Harry Potter and the Source of Inspiration," *Electronic Telegraph,* July 1, 2000).

Yet Rowling, for some reason, claims she knows little about witchcraft and has no real interest in it. "I truly am bemused that anyone who has read the books would think that I am a proponent of the occult in any serious way. I don't believe in witchcraft, in the sense that they're talking about, at all. . . . I don't believe in magic in the way I describe it in my books" ("Success Stuns Harry Potter Author," *Associated Press,* July 6, 2000).

But during a 1999 interview, Rowling was forced to admit that she had studied mythology, witchcraft, and the exact words used in witches spells for the purposes of her novels. During that call-in interview, a self-professed wizard excitedly asked Rowling if she was a member of the "Craft" (or Wicca, an organization of witches). When she answered no, he was shocked. He confessed, "Well, you've done your homework quite well!" He went on to say that he loved the Potter books because they were full of the same occult formulas he regularly used.

Regardless of the claims made by Rowling, three facts seem certain:

1. The *Harry Potter* series both teaches and glorifies witchcraft,
2. Her series is one of the most popular of all time, taking the world by storm, and,
3. Christians are enthralled by Rowling books.
4. Those who condemn the books are mocked as religious nutcases, much like the characters who reject witchcraft in the book.

As you have come to understand the reality of life after death and what happens when we die, do you see clearly the dangers of the occult and spiritualism? It is obvious that much of America doesn't . . . and for whatever reasons, those who clamor against the kind of evil actively celebrated by Hollywood are cast off as religious bigots.

So the question is, what will you do in light of the evidence? If you choose to reject the Bible's word on this subject, how easy will it be for you to be deceived in areas that really might determine your eternal destiny?

If you stand for the words of God, then God will stand with you. But also know that if you choose this path, to stand against error, the battle before you will not be easy. There is a reason why people are so confused about the spirit world and life after death.

The Battle Over Truth

Those who oppose the teachings of spiritualism are wrestling not only with men, but with Satan and his angels. They have entered upon a contest against principalities, powers and wicked spirits in high places.

Satan will not yield one inch of ground except as he is driven back by the power of heavenly messengers. The people of God should be able to meet him, as did our Savior, with the words, "It is written." Satan can quote Scripture now as in the days of Christ, and he will pervert its teachings to sustain his delusions. Those who would stand in this time of peril must understand for themselves the testimony of the Scriptures. Many will be confronted by the spirits of devils who, in addition to impersonating beloved relatives or friends, declare the most dangerous heresies.

These "spiritual" visitors will appeal to our tenderest sympathies, even working miracles to sustain their pretensions. We must be prepared to withstand them with the Bible truth that the dead know not anything and that they who thus appear are the spirits of devils.

The popular television show *Medium* is based on the "true-life" story of a psychic who helps solves murders and other crimes that are beyond the reach of law enforcement. Yet according to the Bible, the dead know not anything, so to whom exactly is this medium speaking? Can you think of any reason why a demon might be truly helpful to a person in one area, while having ulterior motives in another?

Just before us is "the hour of temptation, which shall come upon all the world, to try them that dwell upon the earth" (Revelation 3:10). All whose faith is not firmly established upon the Word of God will be deceived and overcome.

Satan "works with all deceivableness of unrighteousness" to gain control of the children of men, and his deceptions will continually increase. But he can only gain his object if men voluntarily yield to his temptations.

Those who earnestly seek a knowledge of the truth and are striving to purify their souls through obedience, thus doing what they can to prepare for the conflict, will find, in the God of truth, a sure defense. "Because thou hast kept the word of My patience, I also will keep thee" is the Savior's promise. God would sooner send every angel out of heaven to protect His people than leave one soul who trusts in Him to be overcome by Satan.

The prophet Isaiah foretold the fearful deception that will come upon the wicked, causing them to count themselves secure from the judgments of God: "We have made a covenant with death, and with hell are we at agreement; when the overflowing scourge shall pass through, it shall not come unto us: for we have made lies our refuge, and under falsehood have we hid ourselves" (Isaiah 28:15).

The people Isaiah describes include those who, in their stubborn impenitence, comfort themselves with the assurance that sinners will not be punished. These people believe that all mankind, no matter how corrupt, will become as the angels of God.

Another class of people renounce the truths that heaven has provided as a defense for the righteous in the day of trouble, and accept the refuge of lies offered by Satan in his stead—the delusive pretensions of spiritualism. Such people are making a covenant with death and an agreement with hell—even more emphatically than those who deceive themselves into believing that sinners will not be punished.

The blindness of people of this generation is marvelous beyond expression. Thousands reject the Word of God as unworthy of belief, then, with eager confidence, receive the deceptions of Satan.

Skeptics and scoffers denounce the bigotry of those who contend for the faith of prophets and apostles. They divert themselves from the truth by holding the solemn declarations of the Scriptures concerning Christ and the plan of salvation, and the retribution to be visited upon the rejecters of the truth—up to ridicule.

They profess to have great pity for minds so narrow, weak, and superstitious as to acknowledge the claims of God and obey the requirements of His law. They manifest as much assurance as if, indeed, they had erected an impassable, impenetrable barrier between themselves and the vengeance of God.

Nothing can arouse their fears. So fully have they yielded to the tempter, so closely are they united with him, and so thoroughly imbued with his spirit, that they have no power and no inclination to break away from his snare.

A Masterpiece of Deception

Satan has long been preparing for his final effort to deceive the world. The foundation of his work was laid by the assurance given to Eve in Eden: "Ye shall not surely die." "In the day ye eat thereof, then your eyes shall be opened, and ye shall be as gods, knowing good and evil" (Genesis 3:4, 5). Little by little he has prepared the way for his masterpiece of deception in the development of spiritualism.

Satan has not yet reached the full accomplishment of his designs, but it will be reached in the last remnant of time. Says the prophet, "I saw three unclean spirits like frogs; . . . they are the spirits of devils, working miracles, which go forth unto the kings of the earth and of the whole world, to gather them to the battle of that great day of God Almighty" (Revelation 16:13, 14).

The whole world—except for those who are kept by the power of God through faith in His Word—will be swept into the ranks of this delusion. The people are fast being lulled to a fatal security, to be awakened only by the outpouring of the wrath of God.

It would be well for us, in these last days, to consider the warning of God through the prophet Isaiah: "Judgment also will I lay to the line, and righteousness to the plummet: and the hail shall sweep away the refuge of lies, and the waters shall overflow the hiding place. And your covenant with death shall be disannulled, and your agreement with hell shall not stand; when the overflowing scourge shall pass through, then ye shall be trodden down by it" (Isaiah 28:17, 18).

Final Thought

You've come to the end of an incredible journey. I hope that you have read this book carefully and prayerfully. If you still have questions about the afterlife and the spirit world, take time to reread the parts where you're confused and test them with Scripture.

Remember that not every truth on a subject in the Bible is in one place. You have to look "here a little, there a little, line upon line, and precept upon precept" (Isaiah 28:10). Once you have all the information on a subject in the Bible, take the principles as a whole. Prayerfully consider the weight of evidence, and trust that God will show you the truth.

Satan knows his time is short. He's doing everything possible to make people stumble away from God and trust in things that will lead to eternal loss. If he can get you to believe a lie, you will do his bidding and ultimately lose your soul.

But right now, you have the knowledge to put up an effective defense against his deceptions. You have all the information you need to understand the truth about the spirit world and the afterlife. ✔

Don't sell yourself short. Don't let pride get in the way of truth. This master deception for the end of time will convince many to willingly accept eternal death. You don't have to be one of them.

And finally, do your friends, family, and neighbors an important favor they will never forget—not through the ceaseless ages of eternity. Please help spread this message by sharing this book with others. Change lives . . . Don't put it off!